The Hidden Power
Metatron and the Secret Path
Luiz Santos

Copyright © 2023 Luiz Santos
All rights reserved.
No part of this book may be reproduced in any form or by any means without written permission from the copyright holder.
Cover image © Vellaz Studio
Review by Marco Villar
Graphic design by Clara Mendonça
Layout by Ricardo Almeida
All rights reserved to:
Luiz A. Santos
Category: Holism

Summary

Prologue 4
Chapter 1 Spiritual Introduction 8
Chapter 2 Fundamental Chakras 14
Chapter 3 Higher Chakras 20
Chapter 4 Energy and Vibration 27
Chapter 5 Meditation with Metatron 34
Chapter 6 Energy Cleansing 41
Chapter 7 Spiritual Protection 48
Chapter 8 Expansion of Consciousness 55
Chapter 9 Positive Manifestation 62
Chapter 10 Life Purpose 69
Chapter 11 Spiritual Self-Healing 76
Chapter 12 Connection with Nature 83
Chapter 13 Intuition and Wisdom 90
Chapter 14 Chakra Cleansing 98
Chapter 15 Energy Alignment 105
Chapter 16 Advanced Meditation 109
Chapter 17 Chakras and Emotions 117
Chapter 18 Dream Work 124
Chapter 19 Action and Karma 131
Chapter 20 Spiritual Realization 138
Chapter 21 Manifestation 145
Chapter 22 Spiritual Self-Care 152
Chapter 23 Gratitude and Abundance 159
Chapter 24 Aura Strengthening 166

Chapter 25 Spiritual Service 173
Chapter 26 Connection with Ancestors 180
Chapter 27 Overcoming Blockages 187
Chapter 28 Spiritual Rebirth 193
Chapter 29 Wisdom Integration 198
Chapter 30 Peace and Contentment 204
Chapter 31 Final Connection 211
Epilogue 216

Prologue

In the space between what you know as tangible reality and what you only sense, a unique force waits, silent, ready to guide your journey. This book has not arrived in your life by chance; it is a gateway. By opening it, you initiate an ancient dance of energy and intuition, led by Archangel Metatron—a luminous guide transcending the limitations of time and space. His role, veiled in mystery, is to take you to the core of a profound spiritual wisdom woven between visible and invisible realms.

Metatron appears as one who has walked this path before, ascending from human to angelic being, and now he invites you to do the same: to rediscover and realign your spiritual essence. He is not just a distant guide but a constant, transformative presence, gently preparing each step you will take on this inward quest. As you take in each page, you will find a call that reaches beyond the common boundaries of understanding. This presence draws near to unveil what the conscious mind often overlooks—the existence of a universal energy flowing through everything and everyone, connecting each being, pulsing in each thought, nourishing every soul.

In this moment, Metatron invites you to tune into the subtle current that permeates the universe. This energy is not something ethereal or intangible; it manifests in each heartbeat, in every inhale and exhale, and in the peace that emerges when you consciously surrender to it. However, this surrender requires you to transcend old beliefs and rigid patterns, as if, through advancing in this text, you were gradually shedding unnecessary burdens, preparing yourself to feel energy in its fullness.

The journey awaiting you in the following pages is not one of ready answers; on the contrary, it suggests a path to be traveled, a gradual uncovering of inner truths. Metatron, the energy emanating from this book, guides you in building a deeper understanding of your own energy centers—your chakras—and how they are gateways that lead to the true balance between body and spirit. These portals open one by one, connecting you to the divine that resides both within and around you.

As you read, you will be led to explore each chakra as a living center of energy, carrying wisdom accumulated over generations. Each energy center helps you access deeper layers of yourself, and as you progress, you will feel a subtle yet powerful transformation unfolding within. This work is a compass to help you align with this vital flow, dissolving blockages, heightening perception, and enabling an uninterrupted communication between your physical being and spiritual essence.

Metatron teaches you that in silence and introspection, unexpected revelations arise like lights illuminating the path. They are not forced ideas; they come from within, like memories surfacing from forgetfulness, reminders of a connection that was always there but had been concealed by the frantic pace of modern life. This book invites you to reconnect with that link and expand it, linking you not only to your own energy but to the universal web of life, where every being and every energy vibrates in harmony.

Each chapter is a step on this path of energetic alignment, not a simple practical guide. It is not about understanding the chakras in an abstract way, but about feeling them in action, noticing their influence in every thought, emotion, and decision. As you journey through these teachings, you will become a receptive channel, able to perceive not only what surrounds you but what emanates from within—the impact of every intention and choice.

Throughout this journey, you will discover that Archangel Metatron offers a unique gift: a spiritual practice that integrates body and soul, that grounds and expands, a way of living that allows you to walk with firmness yet never stop soaring. The techniques and reflections presented are not only for your individual benefit; they are keys that open collective consciousness, revealing the harmony that exists when each of us aligns with our own truth.

In this process of harmonization and connection, you will learn that energy is not merely a concept but a tangible state of being. Metatron will guide you to experience universal energy as something that renews, protects, and elevates. Every suggested practice in the book—each visualization and meditation—is an invitation for you to embrace this energetic reality as an integral part of your life, blending it into every action, every gesture, every word.

Prepare to set aside the distractions and limitations of the external world, to immerse yourself in an experience of reunion with your essence. The wisdom contained here is not theoretical; it manifests in practice, in the exercises that invite you to make direct contact with your own energy and to rediscover the hidden power you carry. This is an invitation for you, the chosen reader, to embrace the opportunity to tread a path of self-discovery, healing, and growth.

From the moment you accept this book's invitation, you enter a sacred space, a place of continuous discoveries where the unknown does not generate fear but fascination. It is in this space that Metatron's words echo, each carrying the promise of a deeper understanding and a more vivid, conscious presence. Let yourself be guided, for this is only the beginning of an awakening that, at some level, you have long awaited.

Chapter 1
Spiritual Introduction

In the quiet spaces between thought and emotion, in the silence that exists beyond words, spirituality begins its slow, transformative dance. And at the core of this dance, Archangel Metatron steps forward, a luminous guide, leading us into realms of understanding that surpass the material. Metatron, whose roots lie in ancient mystical traditions, holds a unique position within the cosmic hierarchy, often described as the scribe of the divine, the intermediary who speaks the language of the heavens and the earth. His energy, powerful and purposeful, offers a key to bridging these dimensions, allowing those who seek to transcend the limitations of the physical world and perceive the boundless landscape of spiritual reality.

In Kabbalistic wisdom, Metatron embodies an intricate blend of divine power and earthly insight, embodying the balance between realms. It is said that he was once human, known as Enoch, before ascending to the angelic, thus serving as a perfect bridge between the human experience and the divine order. Through his transformation, he became a symbol of what is possible when one aligns with a higher purpose and universal energies. This alignment is at the heart of spiritual awakening—a process that Metatron guides with clarity and patience. He invites each of us to resonate with the energies that shape existence, to listen beyond the noise, and to feel the rhythm of life in every breath.

Aligning with universal energy is like entering a cosmic river, a stream that flows through all living things, connecting every soul with the Source. This energy is not distant or abstract; it is as close as the heartbeat, as constant as the cycles of nature. Through Metatron, one learns to tune into this current, to sense it within and around, and to realize that every individual soul is a unique part of this interconnected web. When one begins to consciously engage with this energy, a shift occurs. There is a shedding of the old, a clearing of rigid patterns and beliefs, making room for a deeper connection with the essence of the self. Here lies the doorway to an authentic spiritual journey.

As Metatron's energy surrounds and supports, the seeker starts to perceive the qualities necessary to cultivate spiritual alignment. Patience, humility, and openness become the pillars of this practice, supporting a heart willing to embrace both the beauty and the mystery of the path. Unlike earthly achievements, which often demand force or control, the spiritual path that Metatron illuminates encourages gentle receptivity, where surrender becomes a powerful tool. Surrendering does not mean giving up but rather aligning one's desires and intentions with a wisdom greater than the individual ego, allowing universal energy to flow without obstruction.

One might begin this alignment in the simplest of ways— through moments of quiet reflection, an intentional breath, or a focused meditation on the energy Metatron brings forth. This energy has a texture that is both grounding and elevating, rooting the individual in the present moment while opening them to divine consciousness. It is like standing on the shore of an endless ocean, with waves of insight gently washing over, each wave deepening the understanding of interconnectedness and purpose. Such moments create a shift from merely existing to truly living in harmony with one's highest self.

As Metatron leads the seeker into this state of receptivity, he also encourages clarity about intentions. Why does one seek? What drives this thirst for understanding? These questions are not meant to limit but to deepen the journey. Each answer reveals layers of the self, exposing both strengths and shadows, both of which are essential parts of the journey. With each discovery,

Metatron's guidance offers reassurance that there is a place and purpose for every part of the self within the greater whole. The seeker learns that alignment with universal energy is not a linear path but a continuous, evolving process that unfolds through every thought, action, and choice.

In this beginning phase, a subtle transformation takes place. What was once fragmented within starts to unify, as though pieces of an intricate puzzle are finding their place. This alignment nurtures inner peace, an understanding that there is a reason for every moment, every experience, every connection. Metatron's presence is both a reminder and a catalyst for this alignment. He whispers to the soul, urging it to step into its full power, to resonate with the truth that it carries within.

Through this process, the seeker is introduced to a new way of being—one that transcends the rush and distractions of ordinary life. Daily interactions and responsibilities no longer feel disconnected from spiritual purpose but become part of a larger pattern, each encounter an opportunity to practice alignment and presence. This perspective fosters a life that flows in tune with universal energy, a life where the sacred and the mundane coexist seamlessly. In such a state, even the simplest of actions hold deeper meaning, as they are performed with awareness and a sense of contribution to the collective whole.

Ultimately, the essence of Metatron's teachings in this introduction is not about escape from the world but about deeper immersion within it, through the lens of spiritual understanding. It is a call to engage with life from a place of inner clarity and peace, knowing that there is guidance available, wisdom woven into every experience. Through Metatron, one learns that spirituality is not confined to the realms of meditation or prayer but is a way of life—a continuous alignment with the flow of existence, a recognition of one's place within the vast, unfolding story of the universe.

Each step along this path is infused with purpose, each moment a stepping stone toward awakening. By following Metatron's guidance, the seeker opens to a journey that is as eternal as it is personal, where growth and discovery never cease, and where every insight is both a destination and a doorway to even greater understanding. In Metatron's light, the journey of spiritual alignment becomes a radiant path, one that illuminates the way to the soul's true home in the boundless realms of the divine.

The journey with Archangel Metatron deepens, drawing the seeker into a landscape where the energies of the body and spirit harmonize, and the barriers between realms begin to dissolve. Metatron's presence becomes more than guidance; it is an invitation to awaken the dormant centers within, a call to align the inner self with the greater, unseen energy that flows through all things. As Metatron's influence radiates through the heart, mind, and soul, the understanding of chakra alignment emerges as an essential step on this journey. Each energy center, each chakra, resonates with the divine, serving as both a beacon and a mirror, reflecting the soul's path to wholeness.

Chakras are not simply points of energy; they are portals that connect the physical, mental, and spiritual dimensions, guiding the flow of life force within. Through them, we interact with the subtle layers of existence, absorbing and radiating energies that shape our experiences, emotions, and thoughts. Metatron's role in harmonizing these centers is profound. His energy operates like a compass, realigning these wheels of energy toward balance, inviting us to connect more deeply with the divine flow. As the seeker attunes to Metatron's guidance, they discover that alignment is not a one-time achievement but an evolving process that resonates in different layers of consciousness and in every aspect of life.

The root, sacral, and solar plexus chakras serve as the foundation, grounding the individual in stability, creativity, and personal power. But to transcend and truly experience a spiritual awakening, one must continue upward, tuning into the heart, throat, third eye, and crown chakras. These higher chakras are the doors to deeper spiritual awareness, and it is here that Metatron's influence can be felt most profoundly. With each breath of alignment, the seeker finds clarity and stillness, a state where the mind's chatter softens, and a deeper voice begins to speak—a voice attuned to wisdom and understanding.

Metatron's guidance allows these chakras to harmonize as a singular pathway, where the energies flow like an undisturbed river from the root to the crown. This flow fosters a sense of purpose, a quiet confidence that one is aligned with something greater than oneself. As the seeker experiences this alignment, a new awareness unfolds. They begin to sense how each chakra not only supports the individual but also connects them to others and the universe itself. This interconnectedness becomes a profound truth, revealing the oneness that exists beneath the surface of ordinary life, a fabric woven by Metatron's hand, carrying divine purpose.

With each step along this path, there is a softening of the soul's defenses, a release of the burdens that once weighed down the spirit. Energies that were once blocked now flow with ease, reshaping the inner landscape to one of openness, love, and acceptance. The chakras, once dormant or disrupted by unresolved emotions, begin to resonate harmoniously, creating a sense of inner peace that is reflected in the outer world. Life's challenges are not removed, but they are seen through a new lens—each moment becomes an opportunity for spiritual alignment, a chance to respond with grace and awareness.

As Metatron guides this alignment, the seeker realizes that chakra harmony does not only bring personal healing but radiates into all areas of life, influencing relationships, health, creativity, and decision-making. In this state of alignment, the spiritual and material realms merge effortlessly. Daily actions become part of the spiritual journey, and every interaction becomes an opportunity to express the higher self. This integrated approach allows the seeker to experience life as a spiritual practice, where growth and expansion are constant, where learning and humility are embraced.

The journey with Metatron is not a solitary one; his energy is a reminder of the support that exists for all who seek it. He stands as a guardian and teacher, guiding the seeker through the layers of self, helping them to peel back the layers that mask true identity. Through his presence, the seeker gains access to energies that illuminate hidden parts of the self, showing where healing is needed and where growth can flourish. In this way, Metatron prepares the seeker not only to understand their own energy centers but to use this knowledge to bring light and alignment to others as well, creating a ripple effect of spiritual elevation.

As the seeker aligns with the energy of Metatron, they are prepared for the deeper practices that follow. In this state, the chakras serve not merely as points of energy but as instruments for transformation, each one tuned to a divine frequency that resonates with universal love and wisdom. This attunement is not only the beginning of spiritual alignment but the foundation upon which all future practices will build. Through this foundation, the seeker is ready to journey further, to open each chakra fully and let the divine energy flow through in a continuous dance of enlightenment and inner peace.

Chapter 2
Fundamental Chakras

Deep within each of us lies an intricate network of energy centers, waiting to be awakened, balanced, and aligned. Known as chakras, these centers govern not only the physical and spiritual aspects of our being but also serve as the energetic foundations upon which higher consciousness and self-realization rest. The journey into these centers of power begins with the three fundamental chakras: the root, sacral, and solar plexus. Together, they anchor us to the earth, infuse us with creativity, and ignite our inner strength.

The root chakra, or Muladhara, sits at the base of the spine. It is our connection to survival, security, and the physical body, grounding us in the material world. Often visualized as a vibrant red wheel, this chakra embodies the essence of stability and safety. It is the foundation of all other chakras, for without a stable root, the energy cannot effectively rise to the higher centers. When balanced, the root chakra instills a profound sense of belonging and a fearlessness that allows us to face life's challenges. Yet, when out of alignment, this chakra becomes the birthplace of insecurity, anxiety, and a sense of rootlessness.

The sacral chakra, or Svadhisthana, resides just below the navel, glowing with a fiery orange hue that embodies the essence of creativity, sexuality, and pleasure. Here, we encounter the energy that fuels our passions, drives our creative endeavors, and allows for the free expression of emotions. When the sacral chakra is balanced, one experiences a fluidity of thought and feeling, an openness to life's pleasures, and a freedom in relationships. However, blockages in this chakra can lead to suppressed emotions, difficulty in connecting with others, and a stagnation of creative energy. It is here that the journey of self-expression and emotional balance begins.

Above the sacral, shining like the sun, is the solar plexus chakra, or Manipura. Often envisioned as a radiant yellow energy, this chakra governs personal power, confidence, and determination. It is the center of one's identity and self-worth, the place from which we take bold steps toward our goals. The solar plexus enables us to stand tall, embracing our unique identity and the purpose that drives us forward. When in harmony, the solar plexus empowers with clarity, inner strength, and the will to act. But in dissonance, it can give rise to self-doubt, feelings of inadequacy, and a tendency to feel powerless.

Each of these foundational chakras is a mirror of our internal landscape, reflecting not only our inner beliefs but the influence of our outer world as well. When these centers are aligned, they become channels for energy to rise, feeding and empowering the higher chakras. The root keeps us grounded, the sacral fuels our passion, and the solar plexus ignites our courage. Together, they form a triad of strength, resilience, and creativity—a trio that supports every endeavor, every emotion, and every pursuit.

The harmony of these chakras does not come automatically but requires conscious effort and attention. Balancing them begins with awareness: paying attention to one's feelings, thoughts, and behaviors that might indicate an imbalance. An individual may feel disconnected from the body, creatively blocked, or plagued by doubt—each of these sensations a sign that energy flow in one of the chakras is disrupted. However, with awareness comes the ability to heal, allowing energy to circulate freely and fully, replenishing each center with vitality.

In this journey of chakra alignment, Metatron's presence offers a unique support. His energy, often visualized as a brilliant, geometric light, is an aid to grounding and strengthening these centers. The seeker can visualize Metatron's energy flowing through each chakra, clearing out the stagnant energies and imbuing them with divine light. The root chakra connects deeply with Metatron's stabilizing presence, grounding the individual in both the earth and the spiritual realms. This grounding provides a sense of security that extends beyond physical reality, touching a spiritual certainty that remains unaffected by external events.

As the seeker moves upward, the sacral chakra welcomes Metatron's influence to rekindle the spark of creativity and joy. This is where the joy of existence is rediscovered—the ability to enjoy life's simple moments, to create without fear, and to embrace one's true nature. When connected to Metatron, this chakra illuminates our unique gifts and the ways in which we can express them authentically in the world. It encourages us to live fully, to explore our depths, and to create without inhibition.

At the solar plexus, Metatron's energy strengthens the will, enhancing confidence and clarity. Here, the seeker can visualize Metatron's light as a golden flame, empowering them to step into their power without fear. This alignment fosters an unwavering sense of self-respect, one that does not waver under external pressures. Through Metatron's guidance, the solar plexus chakra becomes a beacon of inner strength, illuminating the path ahead with courage and purpose.

The power of these foundational chakras lies not only in their individual functions but in their collective synergy. Together, they offer a solid foundation upon which the seeker can build, creating a balanced and resilient energy system that supports every level of consciousness. This grounding prepares the seeker to explore the higher chakras, where intuition, expression, and divine connection come into play. But without this foundational strength, the higher centers cannot be fully activated.

As the root, sacral, and solar plexus chakras align under Metatron's guidance, the seeker stands prepared for deeper exploration, equipped with resilience, creativity, and inner power. This is the groundwork of spiritual growth, a place of stability from which the soul can soar. In this state, life itself becomes a meditation, an act of alignment, where each choice reflects the harmony within. Through Metatron's influence, the seeker becomes a channel for universal energy, grounded in strength, inspired by creativity, and driven by purpose, ready to rise into higher realms of consciousness.

The path of aligning the root, sacral, and solar plexus chakras is not one of instant transformation but of dedicated practice, requiring both intention and surrender. As these foundational energy centers stabilize, the journey gains depth, guided by Archangel Metatron, who imparts the wisdom and strength necessary to release stagnant energies and to awaken the full potential of these chakras. Each center holds within it patterns, memories, and emotions that shape one's identity, and only through conscious work can they be rebalanced, opening the seeker to a profound sense of inner harmony.

One of the simplest yet most powerful practices for grounding the root chakra begins with visualization. The seeker is invited to sit quietly, feet flat on the ground, and to imagine roots growing from the base of their spine, deep into the earth. In this moment, Archangel Metatron's presence can be felt as a wave of warmth and reassurance, as though he is holding a sacred space for grounding. This practice encourages the energy of the root chakra to anchor securely, releasing anxiety and deepening the feeling of safety. When practiced daily, this grounding exercise serves as a powerful tool for cultivating stability and resilience, making one more receptive to the divine flow in everyday life.

The sacral chakra, seat of creativity and joy, benefits greatly from movement. Dance, even in its simplest form, becomes a way to connect with the inner creative force that resides in this center. As the body moves, the sacral energy flows more freely, dissolving tension and opening pathways for self-expression. Here, Metatron's guidance can be visualized as a radiant orange light that moves through the lower abdomen, restoring passion and creativity. Through this movement, there is an invitation to let go of restrictions, to allow emotions to be felt without judgment, and to trust in the wisdom that arises from this process. It is a reminder that creativity is a divine gift, one that reflects the universal energy in each individual's unique way of being.

For the solar plexus chakra, the energy center of confidence and willpower, focused breathing is especially powerful. The seeker can place their hands over the area just above the navel and breathe deeply, imagining a golden light growing stronger with each breath. This light, representing the inner fire, strengthens the sense of purpose and clears away self-doubt. As Metatron's presence is called upon, his golden light amplifies this personal power, filling the solar plexus with warmth and courage. This practice awakens the conviction to act with integrity, aligning one's choices with the soul's highest purpose. In time, the solar plexus becomes a wellspring of strength and direction, empowering the seeker to move through life with clarity.

The process of aligning these chakras under Metatron's guidance invites an awareness of the connections between body, mind, and spirit. It is a daily renewal, where small practices evolve into powerful habits, infusing each moment with consciousness. Simple actions, like mindful walking or even pausing to take a few grounded breaths throughout the day, become acts of alignment. Over time, these practices dissolve barriers within, making space for spiritual energy to flow effortlessly from the root to the higher chakras. The seeker begins to feel a calm strength, a subtle shift where fear and doubt no longer hold sway.

In addition to visualizations and breathing exercises, the seeker may incorporate rituals of protection and grounding, using elements like crystals to reinforce each chakra's stability. Red jasper or hematite can be held during grounding exercises to amplify the root chakra's energy, while carnelian enhances the sacral chakra's vibrancy. For the solar plexus, citrine offers an energizing and purifying force, amplifying personal power and resilience. When paired with Metatron's energy, these stones serve as reminders of the sacred work being undertaken, aligning the seeker's physical and spiritual dimensions in harmony.

Metatron's guidance creates a deepening awareness that alignment is not merely a matter of individual well-being but is also a bridge to collective harmony. Each aligned chakra becomes a channel for transmitting peace, compassion, and balance into the world. In Metatron's light, this journey is recognized as an act of service, a gift to the collective as well as to oneself. The energies that flow through these centers are interconnected with the energies of others, creating a network of spiritual alignment that uplifts not only the individual but the greater consciousness of humanity.

The cumulative effect of these practices is a newfound resilience—a steady, empowered presence in the face of life's challenges. The root, sacral, and solar plexus chakras, once fragmented or blocked, now work as a unified force, grounding the seeker in purpose and possibility. Through this harmony, Metatron's wisdom begins to permeate every aspect of daily life. Relationships improve, creativity flows without effort, and decisions are made with confidence and trust in one's path. With each breath, each visualization, and each act of grounding, the seeker forges a foundation that will support them through deeper spiritual explorations.

In this state of alignment, life is no longer a series of random events but a deeply interconnected journey guided by purpose and intention. Metatron's light, now woven into the seeker's core, shines brightly, illuminating the path forward with wisdom and clarity. The alignment of the root, sacral, and solar plexus chakras forms a sacred triad of stability, creativity, and strength, empowering the seeker to embrace life's mysteries with an open heart and a grounded soul. This foundation is not an end but a beginning, the groundwork upon which higher spiritual realms will be explored, carrying the seeker ever closer to the divine essence within.

Chapter 3
Higher Chakras

As the seeker ascends through the energetic centers, leaving behind the foundational roots, the journey unfolds into the realms of the higher chakras. These energy centers—the heart, throat, third eye, and crown—are bridges between the human experience and the divine, channels that allow intuition, truth, and spiritual wisdom to flow. Here, the subtle realms become vibrant, the soul opens, and consciousness begins to touch the sacred. With Archangel Metatron's presence as a steady guide, these chakras awaken to their fullest potential, expanding the boundaries of perception and bringing the seeker closer to a state of spiritual alignment that transcends the ordinary.

The heart chakra, or Anahata, sits at the center of this journey, a meeting point between the physical and spiritual realms. Often visualized as a soft, emerald-green light, it is here that love, compassion, and forgiveness blossom. In this space, the seeker learns to transcend the self and embrace the unity of all beings. The heart chakra opens the soul to the truth that each individual is both unique and inseparably connected to others. Under Metatron's guidance, this center glows with unconditional love, inviting the seeker to release old wounds, to let go of resentments, and to embody a love that is as boundless as it is profound.

Metatron's influence helps the heart chakra heal and expand, creating a space where both earthly and divine love reside. Visualizing Metatron's light filling the heart center, the seeker may feel a gentle warmth or a deep calm that radiates outward, dissolving fears of vulnerability or rejection. Through this openness, the heart becomes a vessel for divine energy, a channel that nurtures all relationships and interactions. Here, one finds not only self-love but a compassion that extends effortlessly to all living beings. This connection to universal love forms the essence of spiritual awakening, a state where the heart knows that all of existence is interconnected.

The journey then rises to the throat chakra, or Vishuddha, a sky-blue sphere of energy located at the throat. This chakra governs expression, truth, and the courage to speak one's authentic voice. In a world filled with noise and superficial words, the throat chakra invites the seeker to cultivate silence, to listen deeply, and to find words that resonate with the truth of the soul. Metatron's energy assists in clearing this chakra, allowing for the release of fears that suppress authentic expression. As the seeker visualizes Metatron's light filling the throat, there is a softening, a release of the need for approval, and an emergence of clarity in communication.

In this alignment, words become sacred. Each thought and intention behind speech is chosen with care, reflecting inner integrity and compassion. The throat chakra, guided by Metatron, becomes not just a center of expression but a bridge between the heart's wisdom and the world. Speaking truth becomes a way to honor both the self and others, an act that enhances inner peace and strengthens one's presence. This chakra, when in harmony, gives the seeker the ability to express their highest truth and to listen with empathy, creating a dialogue that uplifts and connects.

From the throat, the journey ascends to the third eye, or Ajna chakra, seated at the brow between the eyes. Represented by a deep indigo light, this chakra is the seat of intuition, insight, and inner vision. It is through the third eye that the seeker begins to see beyond the illusions of the material world, to sense the deeper truths that lie beneath the surface. Metatron's influence at this center is transformative, opening the inner eye to divine wisdom and heightening the ability to perceive subtle energies. As his light flows through this chakra, the seeker may begin to experience flashes of insight, heightened awareness, or a sense of clarity about life's mysteries.

The third eye chakra reveals the interconnectedness of all things, a perception that transcends logic and rests in intuition. Metatron's guidance here allows the seeker to trust in their inner knowing, to release doubts that cloud perception, and to embrace a deeper understanding of reality. This connection to intuitive wisdom is a powerful tool on the spiritual path, revealing a world that operates beyond physical sight. Through this inner vision, the seeker learns to navigate life with an awareness that aligns with the soul's highest intentions.

At the crown of this journey lies the crown chakra, or Sahasrara, a radiant violet or white light that connects the individual to the divine source. This chakra, located just above the head, is the portal through which divine wisdom flows, a doorway to cosmic consciousness. Metatron's energy here is like a beacon, illuminating the seeker's connection to the infinite, to the boundless reality that lies beyond form and thought. With Metatron's presence, the crown chakra opens gently, allowing the seeker to experience a sense of unity, a dissolving of the ego's boundaries, and a recognition of the soul's divine essence.

This is where the individual and the universal meet, where the self merges with the whole, and where a deep peace resides. In the presence of Metatron, the crown chakra becomes a channel for divine energy, an opening through which the seeker connects to the wisdom that lies beyond words. Here, thoughts quiet, and the mind enters a stillness that is vast, serene, and luminous. This state of connection is not an escape from the world but an invitation to engage with it fully, with an awareness that everything, in its essence, is sacred.

These higher chakras—heart, throat, third eye, and crown—form a ladder of consciousness, guiding the seeker from earthly experience to spiritual transcendence. Together, they create a pathway through which Metatron's light flows, illuminating the journey with wisdom, compassion, and clarity. In this alignment, the seeker discovers not only a deeper connection with the self but with all of existence. The higher chakras become vessels for divine energy, carrying Metatron's guidance and wisdom into every thought, word, and action.

As each higher chakra opens, the seeker is reminded of the vastness within, a space where human experience and divine consciousness intertwine. Through the heart, love flows unconditionally; through the throat, truth emerges fearlessly; through the third eye, intuition guides with clarity; and through the crown, unity with the divine is realized. This alignment forms the basis of true spiritual evolution, a journey that is both personal and universal, individual yet profoundly interconnected.

With Metatron's presence illuminating these centers, the seeker is prepared to live in harmony with the divine flow, grounded in the strength of the lower chakras and uplifted by the wisdom of the higher. This state of alignment with the higher chakras is not an end, but a beginning—a doorway into a life lived in full awareness, guided by love, truth, insight, and a deep connection to the sacred. Through Metatron, the path of spiritual alignment becomes not just a journey but a way of being, a path that unfolds infinitely, resonating with the boundless light of the divine.

The awakening of the higher chakras is a transformative journey, and as these energy centers begin to open, the seeker is guided by Archangel Metatron through practices that help each chakra bloom into its fullest potential. Beyond simply opening, these practices encourage the harmonization and integration of each chakra's energy, deepening the connection to divine consciousness and empowering the seeker to live with greater clarity, intuition, and compassion. Under Metatron's guidance, the heart, throat, third eye, and crown chakras resonate not only with individual purpose but with universal truth.

The heart chakra, or Anahata, is the source of boundless love and compassion. To activate this center, Metatron teaches a gentle visualization, guiding the seeker to imagine a soft, green light growing within the heart, expanding outward like the petals of a lotus. With each breath, this light grows, filling the chest, then radiating outward to encompass the entire body. As Metatron's light merges with this heart energy, a powerful shift occurs—a feeling of peace, forgiveness, and deep compassion for oneself and others. Through this practice, the heart chakra is not only opened but is strengthened as a wellspring of love that flows effortlessly into all interactions, nurturing both the self and those around.

With the heart aligned, the journey rises to the throat chakra, or Vishuddha, where Metatron offers practices to enhance truthful expression. To activate this center, the seeker may sit in silence, allowing the breath to become steady and deep. Metatron's light, visualized as a sky-blue hue, is invited to fill the throat, releasing any blockages that suppress expression. With each exhale, the seeker releases self-doubt, fear of judgment, or any lingering insecurities that hinder the authentic voice. Here, Metatron's energy encourages the seeker to speak with honesty and empathy, creating words that bridge understanding and uplift those who listen. In this state of openness, the throat chakra becomes a channel for sharing inner truth, resonating with clarity and integrity.

For the third eye, or Ajna chakra, Metatron guides the seeker into practices of expanded vision and intuition. As the seeker sits in quiet focus, they are encouraged to visualize a deep indigo light at the center of the brow, where intuition rests. Metatron's influence here is profound, awakening the ability to see beyond ordinary perception. Guided visualization allows the seeker to focus on this indigo light, letting it fill the mind, dissolving distractions, and quieting mental chatter. With each breath, the third eye opens further, enhancing the seeker's ability to perceive deeper truths. This practice sharpens intuition, enabling a connection with inner wisdom and providing insight that transcends logical thought. With Metatron's light at the third eye, the seeker begins to trust in their inner vision, finding a clarity that guides decisions and strengthens spiritual awareness.

At the crown chakra, or Sahasrara, Metatron's guidance leads to an experience of divine unity. To engage this center, the seeker visualizes a radiant violet or pure white light above the head, shining with an intensity that links them to the infinite. In this practice, the seeker surrenders completely, allowing Metatron's light to merge with their own, filling the entire being with a luminous energy. The crown chakra expands, opening to the vastness of divine wisdom, a state where thoughts fade, and a profound sense of unity is felt. In this meditative space, the seeker experiences the peace and vastness of universal consciousness, a realization that they are part of a greater whole, a connection that transcends individuality and merges into the divine.

Together, these practices for the higher chakras bring the seeker to a place of profound spiritual alignment. Metatron's influence weaves through each energy center, creating a harmonious flow that connects the body, mind, and spirit to the larger universal energy. The heart chakra radiates love, the throat chakra speaks truth, the third eye perceives wisdom, and the crown chakra unites with the divine. This state of alignment is both grounding and transcendent, a sacred balance that empowers the seeker to live with purpose and compassion.

Through daily commitment to these practices, the higher chakras become vessels for Metatron's wisdom, allowing divine energy to flow into all aspects of life. The seeker's presence becomes a calming force, their words resonate with authenticity, and their vision guides them with intuitive clarity. Each action, each thought, each breath becomes part of a larger dance with the divine, where the individual is both grounded in the self and open to the universe.

This connection to the higher chakras is not only a path to self-realization but a channel through which divine wisdom flows into the world. Metatron's guidance ensures that this awakening remains anchored, a steady and gentle expansion that supports the seeker's growth and inspires those they encounter. In this state, the seeker begins to see life itself as a spiritual practice, each moment a meditation on alignment, each interaction an opportunity to express the sacred within.

Through the practices Metatron offers, the seeker learns to cultivate a life that reflects this alignment. Challenges become lessons, relationships deepen, and the mind settles into a peaceful awareness that extends beyond daily concerns. In this harmony, the heart's love, the throat's truth, the third eye's insight, and the crown's unity form a cohesive force, connecting the seeker to a life imbued with spiritual purpose. The alignment of the higher chakras becomes a transformative force, guiding the seeker to live with compassion, wisdom, and an unwavering connection to the divine, an openness that reflects the limitless love and insight Metatron brings to those who seek.

Chapter 4
Energy and Vibration

Energy resonates within and beyond us, shaping each moment, influencing thoughts, emotions, and experiences in ways that often remain unseen but are deeply felt. In this space, Archangel Metatron appears as a guide through the subtle currents of vibrational frequency, revealing how aligning with higher energies brings clarity, spiritual growth, and inner harmony. To grasp vibrational frequency is to understand that each individual vibrates at a unique frequency, a rhythm influenced by thoughts, emotions, and the energies we absorb from the world around us.

Metatron invites the seeker to consider vibration as a reflection of spiritual health. Low frequencies, marked by emotions such as fear, anger, or jealousy, create a dense energy that clouds perception and distorts reality. In contrast, high frequencies, which resonate with joy, love, gratitude, and peace, elevate the spirit and open pathways to a clearer, more connected awareness. With Metatron's guidance, the seeker begins to understand that vibrational frequency is not static; it is a dynamic force, influenced by every thought, feeling, and interaction. This knowledge becomes a tool for conscious living, where intentional thoughts and emotions are cultivated to maintain a higher vibrational state.

The journey into vibrational alignment starts with a shift in awareness. By observing the energies that surround us, from the conversations we engage in to the environments we inhabit, we can begin to see the effects on our internal landscape.

Metatron teaches that awareness is the first step in transformation; it is through understanding and recognizing these influences that one can begin to choose alignment over dissonance. In this way, raising one's frequency becomes a choice—a commitment to nurturing thoughts, emotions, and actions that resonate with the higher self.

Practicing gratitude is among the simplest yet most powerful ways to elevate vibration. Metatron encourages the seeker to start each day with a moment of gratitude, however small or grand the acknowledgment may be. As gratitude grows, so does vibrational resonance, inviting abundance and positive experiences into one's life. When one is aligned with gratitude, there is a palpable shift in energy, a lightness that permeates the mind and spirit, creating an inner peace that radiates outward. This daily practice becomes a foundation, a touchstone that keeps the spirit in a higher vibrational state, regardless of external circumstances.

Metatron also introduces the concept of vibrational tuning through intention. Intentions, like tuning forks, vibrate at specific frequencies and attract energies of a similar nature. By setting intentions aligned with the highest self—be it for peace, love, growth, or understanding—the seeker aligns their energy with universal frequencies that support these intentions. Metatron's light assists in strengthening these vibrations, amplifying intentions and drawing them into reality. This practice encourages a proactive approach to life, where thoughts are consciously chosen, and energy is directed with purpose and clarity.

Metatron guides the seeker to tune into the energy of nature, a powerful source of high frequency that is always available. The vibrational essence of trees, rivers, sunlight, and earth carry a purity that naturally uplifts the spirit. By spending time in nature, walking barefoot on the ground, or simply sitting in silence among trees, one can absorb this frequency, allowing it to cleanse and elevate the spirit. Nature's energy serves as a reminder that high vibration is an inherent part of existence, and through connection with it, the soul realigns with its true essence.

Visualization is another tool Metatron shares for raising vibration. The seeker is encouraged to envision a warm, golden light, vibrating at a high frequency, surrounding and filling their entire being. With each breath, this light grows stronger, dissolving any lingering shadows of fear, resentment, or doubt. Metatron's light joins with this visualization, creating a powerful field of energy that vibrates with peace, joy, and love. This practice not only raises one's frequency but also serves as a shield, protecting the energy field from low vibrations that may arise throughout the day.

With Metatron's guidance, the seeker learns to differentiate between vibrations that elevate and those that deplete. This discernment is essential for maintaining a high vibrational state, as it empowers the individual to choose relationships, environments, and actions that resonate with their spiritual path. In this state of high vibration, life begins to shift. Challenges are met with grace, opportunities align naturally, and interactions are infused with compassion and understanding. This transformation reflects the deeper truth that vibration is not simply a personal experience but a bridge between oneself and the universe, a way of harmonizing with the cosmic rhythm that flows through all things.

Through the alignment of energy and the conscious elevation of vibration, the seeker cultivates a powerful foundation for spiritual growth. Metatron's guidance reveals that raising one's vibrational frequency is not a one-time effort but a continuous practice, a dance with the energies that shape life. Each moment offers an opportunity to elevate, to resonate with a frequency that reflects the soul's highest expression, a state where harmony and inner peace become natural ways of being.

In this heightened state, Metatron's presence becomes more than guidance; it is a resonance, a frequency that aligns with the seeker's own energy, amplifying it and creating a channel for spiritual evolution. Through this process, the seeker learns that vibrational frequency is not only a path to inner peace but a journey into the heart of the universe, a reminder that each thought, feeling, and intention is part of a vast symphony, a melody that connects all things in a dance of light, energy, and purpose.

As the seeker deepens their understanding of vibrational frequency, the journey shifts from awareness to practice. Archangel Metatron, ever a guiding light, reveals techniques that allow one to not only raise personal vibration but to sustain it as a continuous state. Through focused practices involving meditation, crystals, and mantras, the seeker learns to shape their energetic field, transforming daily life into a vessel of spiritual growth. These techniques act as both a shield and a beacon, protecting from lower energies while attracting alignment with higher frequencies that support spiritual evolution.

Meditation serves as one of the most potent tools for elevating vibrational frequency. Under Metatron's guidance, the seeker is introduced to meditative practices that emphasize breath and awareness. Sitting in a quiet space, the seeker closes their eyes, grounding their attention within. Metatron's energy is visualized as a gentle, shimmering light that flows through the crown chakra and fills the entire body, creating a luminous sphere that vibrates with peace and clarity. In this meditative state, the seeker's breath becomes a rhythm that aligns with the higher energies, raising frequency and expanding consciousness. Each inhale invites divine energy, while each exhale releases any lingering negativity, creating a profound sense of inner harmony.

Beyond meditation, the use of crystals offers a tactile, tangible connection to elevated frequencies. Each crystal carries a unique vibrational quality, resonating with particular aspects of the spiritual journey. Metatron's energy harmonizes with stones like amethyst, clear quartz, and selenite, each known for its ability to purify, elevate, and protect. Holding a crystal, the seeker can visualize it as an anchor for Metatron's light, amplifying their intention to connect with higher energies. These stones act as silent guides, each one a small reservoir of universal energy, assisting in keeping the seeker's vibration steady and elevated throughout the day. Placing these crystals near meditation spaces, in personal altars, or even wearing them as jewelry serves as a constant reminder of the vibrational state the seeker aims to maintain.

Mantras further deepen this vibrational work, as sound itself carries powerful frequencies that affect the body, mind, and spirit. Metatron introduces sacred sounds or words that, when spoken or chanted, resonate with high frequencies and align the energy centers. Simple yet powerful, these mantras create vibrations that travel through the seeker's body, dissolving stagnant energy and realigning it with universal harmony. The repetition of these sounds builds a protective and expansive energy field, helping the seeker to remain balanced and focused. Each chant brings the seeker closer to a state of resonance with the divine, connecting not only with Metatron's light but with the vastness of universal consciousness.

In practicing these techniques, the seeker comes to understand that raising frequency is also about releasing attachment to lower vibrations. Emotions such as anger, jealousy, or fear carry dense frequencies that weigh down the spirit, disrupting the natural flow of energy. Metatron teaches that by acknowledging these emotions without attachment—observing them, allowing them to pass—one can prevent them from anchoring in the energy field. In doing so, the seeker cultivates a habit of clearing and renewing their vibrational state, making space for peace, compassion, and joy. Each day becomes an opportunity to refine energy, a ritual of self-awareness and conscious elevation.

Another layer of vibrational practice is the alignment with Metatron's own frequency, which radiates as a protective, purifying force. The seeker learns to call upon Metatron's energy in moments of stress or imbalance, visualizing it as a geometric light, often seen in the form of Metatron's Cube. This sacred symbol spins with potent energy, clearing blockages and elevating the seeker's vibration instantly. By inviting Metatron's presence, the seeker transforms lower energies and creates a shield that preserves their elevated state. Over time, this connection becomes second nature—a constant companion that supports resilience and harmony in the face of life's challenges.

As these practices become integrated, the seeker begins to notice a natural shift in their interactions and experiences. People, opportunities, and environments that resonate with higher vibrations naturally come into alignment, while those that carry lower frequencies begin to fade from view. Life begins to mirror the vibrational state the seeker has cultivated within, reflecting peace, compassion, and understanding. This shift is not merely an internal experience but a transformation of the outer world, where the energy one radiates attracts harmony and balance from the universe.

To maintain this elevated frequency, Metatron guides the seeker in establishing a daily routine that weaves these practices into everyday life. Morning meditations, intentional crystal placement, chanting mantras throughout the day, and nightly reflections on emotions create a rhythm that supports high vibration consistently. This structure not only keeps the seeker aligned with higher energies but also strengthens the bond with Metatron, whose presence grows as a steady light within. Through this consistent practice, the seeker learns that high vibration is both a choice and a commitment, an ongoing dialogue with the universe that asks for presence and devotion.

As the seeker's frequency rises, a new awareness of unity emerges. Metatron reveals that individual vibration does not exist in isolation but as part of a larger, interconnected field. Every thought, action, and intention contributes to the collective frequency, weaving into the energy that shapes the world. In this realization, the seeker's vibrational practice becomes an offering to the greater whole, a conscious participation in elevating not only personal consciousness but the spiritual well-being of all. This collective resonance is the essence of spiritual growth, a harmony that extends beyond the self and into the fabric of the universe itself.

Through these teachings, Metatron imparts that vibrational elevation is not merely a spiritual goal but a way of life—a continual journey of returning to alignment, choosing high frequencies, and embodying the light within. In this elevated state, the seeker becomes a beacon, radiating a calm presence that inspires others to seek their own path of alignment. Guided by Metatron, the seeker learns that true elevation is both personal and universal, a path that honors the sacred in all things and transforms life into a living meditation of resonance, peace, and unity.

Chapter 5
Meditation with Metatron

Meditation, when practiced as a form of communion, offers a path to spiritual awakening, a gateway that connects the seeker to realms of inner clarity and divine understanding. Under the guidance of Archangel Metatron, meditation transforms into more than a calming exercise—it becomes an intentional journey of self-discovery and alignment with universal energy. In this space of quiet introspection, the seeker begins to perceive the subtle energies within, allowing Metatron's light to illuminate hidden truths and unlock dimensions of awareness that transcend the physical.

To begin, Metatron encourages the seeker to establish a dedicated space for meditation, an environment free from distractions, infused with intention. A quiet corner adorned with elements that resonate with the seeker—a candle, a crystal, or an image that reflects their spiritual aspiration—becomes a sacred space. This act of creating a physical setting mirrors the creation of an internal sanctuary, a place within the self where Metatron's presence is welcomed. By setting this intention, the seeker prepares not only the body but also the mind and spirit to enter a state of deep alignment.

As the seeker settles into meditation, they are guided to focus on their breath, allowing each inhale to bring in calmness, and each exhale to release tension. In this rhythm, the mind softens, the body relaxes, and awareness expands. With Metatron's presence, the seeker may visualize a radiant, geometric light—a symbol of divine order and sacred patterns—

enveloping them, forming a protective cocoon. This light, often envisioned as Metatron's Cube, surrounds the seeker with a sense of peace, guarding against distractions and anchoring the spirit in the present moment. It is within this geometric embrace that the seeker feels Metatron's energy, steady and vast, a force that guides them deeper into the silence within.

In this state of quiet, the seeker is invited to turn their awareness inward, to listen not with the ears but with the soul. Here, Metatron's light acts as a catalyst, revealing layers of thoughts and emotions, each one a doorway to self-awareness. By observing these internal states without judgment, the seeker becomes aware of both the strengths and the shadows that reside within. This act of introspection, guided by Metatron, fosters a sense of acceptance and understanding, a gentle reminder that each thought, emotion, and memory has shaped the path leading to this moment.

With each breath, the connection to Metatron deepens. The seeker may feel an energetic warmth in the heart center, a gentle expansion as Metatron's energy harmonizes with their own. In this embrace, meditation becomes a state of communion, where individual concerns fade, replaced by a sense of unity with the divine. Here, Metatron's light penetrates the seeker's being, dissolving fears, doubts, and limitations, filling the inner space with a sense of boundless love and understanding. The mind enters a state of quiet clarity, a calmness that allows the seeker to see beyond everyday concerns, to touch the deeper aspects of the self that yearn for connection.

As this practice unfolds, Metatron introduces the seeker to the art of guided visualization within meditation. Visualizations are not merely imagined scenes but are portals to the spirit, tools for aligning one's intentions and energies with the divine. Metatron might guide the seeker to envision themselves in a place of natural beauty, a landscape of mountains, oceans, or forests, where the energy of the earth merges with their own. In this setting, the seeker is invited to feel the grounding energy of the earth, to sense the connection that binds them to all living things.

This visualization not only strengthens the sense of unity but serves as a foundation, anchoring the seeker's energy in the stability of the natural world.

Beyond grounding, Metatron also guides the seeker in visualizations that awaken higher consciousness. In one such exercise, the seeker may envision a beam of light descending from above, entering through the crown chakra and filling the body with a vibrant energy. This light, symbolizing divine wisdom, flows downward, illuminating each chakra, aligning and harmonizing the entire energy system. With each breath, this light grows brighter, expanding beyond the body to fill the space around, creating an aura of peace and clarity. In this radiant state, the seeker not only experiences personal alignment but becomes aware of their connection to the divine, a reminder that they are a part of something vast and infinite.

As the meditation deepens, the seeker may experience moments of profound stillness, where thoughts quiet and a sense of vastness takes over. These are moments of pure alignment, where the soul resonates fully with Metatron's energy. In this state, wisdom arises not as words but as insights, intuitive understandings that bring clarity and peace. Here, the seeker discovers that meditation is not about achieving silence but about listening to the silence within, where truth and understanding reside beyond the noise of the mind.

Through this practice, Metatron also teaches the seeker the art of grounding after meditation, a vital step to ensure the energies experienced during meditation integrate into daily life. By visualizing roots extending from the base of the spine into the earth, or by placing hands on the ground, the seeker allows any residual energy to flow, creating a stable foundation upon which to carry their newfound awareness. This grounding process ensures that spiritual insights are not lost but are woven into the fabric of daily experience, enriching each moment with the peace and clarity gained in meditation.

Metatron's guidance reveals that meditation is not a solitary act but a bridge between worlds, an invitation to align one's inner landscape with the universal. In these meditative states, the seeker learns that alignment with Metatron's energy is not reserved for moments of stillness but can be carried into all areas of life. Each breath, each quiet moment, each act of mindfulness becomes a continuation of this meditation, a way of honoring the connection that has been forged.

Through these teachings, the seeker's practice transforms. Meditation evolves from a practice into a way of being, where the alignment with Metatron becomes a constant presence, a guide through the complexities of life. This state of inner alignment fosters a peace that extends beyond meditation, a stillness that touches each thought, word, and action. Through Metatron's presence, the seeker discovers that meditation is not a destination but a path, a journey into the heart of the self, where the divine is not a distant reality but an intimate part of every breath, every heartbeat, and every moment.

The path of meditation unfolds further, revealing deeper layers of spiritual connection and awareness. As Archangel Metatron guides the seeker through advanced meditative practices, these moments become more than personal stillness; they are gateways to profound spiritual alignment and insight. Within these deeper states of meditation, the seeker learns to open pathways to the divine, experiencing Metatron's energy as a direct channel that bridges the earthly with the transcendent, allowing for expanded perception and enhanced receptivity.

At the core of these advanced practices lies the art of intentional visualization, where Metatron's presence supports the seeker in crafting vivid, sacred images that resonate with spiritual truth. The seeker, seated comfortably with a quiet mind, begins by visualizing themselves surrounded by a sphere of soft, radiant light, a field created by Metatron's energy. This light, often seen as a gentle yet powerful geometric form, such as Metatron's Cube, vibrates with a frequency that clears distractions and focuses the mind. Within this space, the seeker feels protected, grounded, and aligned, ready to journey inward.

One advanced visualization technique that Metatron introduces involves envisioning a bridge of light, connecting the heart to realms of divine wisdom. As the seeker visualizes this bridge, they are encouraged to walk across it with an open heart, letting go of any resistance or fear. This bridge leads to a vast, serene expanse—a symbol of the boundless spiritual dimension Metatron guides the seeker into. Here, in this space of light, the seeker may feel Metatron's presence intensify, filling them with a quiet strength and profound clarity. This visualization invites the seeker into communion with the higher self, a direct connection where intuitive insights flow freely, unimpeded by the mind's usual filters.

Another transformative technique Metatron guides is the practice of energy harmonization, where the seeker focuses on aligning their chakras with divine energy. In this meditation, the seeker visualizes each chakra as a spinning wheel of light, beginning at the root and rising to the crown. With Metatron's guidance, each chakra is touched by a ray of light, aligning it with the universal flow. This light moves in rhythmic pulses, connecting all centers, creating a channel of energy that flows effortlessly from the base of the spine to the top of the head. As each chakra aligns, the seeker feels a growing sense of wholeness, as though every part of their being resonates with a single, harmonious frequency.

As the seeker grows more comfortable with these practices, Metatron introduces an even deeper form of meditation—a state of pure receptivity. In this space, the seeker is encouraged to let go of all visualizations and intentions, allowing themselves to become an open vessel for whatever arises. This practice requires full trust, a surrendering of control, inviting the divine to communicate in whatever form it may take. With Metatron's support, this meditative state becomes a doorway, an invitation for spiritual guidance, symbols, or visions that may appear unexpectedly. Here, the seeker learns that the deepest truths are not those actively sought but those that reveal themselves in moments of openness and surrender.

One particular technique Metatron offers in this receptive state is the visualization of sacred symbols, forms that appear naturally during meditation and carry unique meanings for the seeker. These symbols may be shapes, colors, or patterns that emerge in the mind's eye, resonating with personal or universal significance. Metatron encourages the seeker to observe these symbols without analysis, simply allowing them to impart their energy and message. Over time, these symbols become personal keys to understanding, tools for navigating the inner world with Metatron's guidance as a trusted interpreter.

With each advanced practice, the seeker's connection to Metatron strengthens, and meditation shifts from an internal process to a direct dialogue with the divine. Metatron's energy becomes a presence that the seeker can feel palpably, a guiding hand that moves through each thought and intention. This connection fosters a deeper peace, a serenity that permeates not only the meditation itself but extends into every aspect of life. Through this ongoing communion, the seeker begins to live with a sustained awareness, an ability to feel Metatron's guidance even outside the moments of stillness.

In time, the seeker may find that meditation with Metatron enhances their ability to perceive the subtle energies that surround them daily. This heightened awareness is not limited to meditation; it becomes an integral part of their perception, an inner compass that guides them through the ebbs and flows of life. Metatron's presence helps the seeker interpret these energies, understanding them as part of a larger tapestry of interconnected experiences. This awareness allows the seeker to respond to challenges with insight, to view relationships with compassion, and to approach each moment as an expression of the divine.

With Metatron's guidance, the seeker is also introduced to grounding techniques after deep meditation, essential practices to bring the expanded awareness back into the physical world. Visualizing roots extending into the earth, feeling the weight of the body, and taking deep, conscious breaths help integrate the spiritual insights gained in meditation. This grounding ensures that the knowledge and peace accessed during meditation are carried forward, allowing the seeker to live in harmony with their highest awareness while remaining fully present in the physical realm.

Through these practices, meditation with Metatron becomes a transformative force, a pathway to a higher state of consciousness that the seeker can access at will. This relationship with Metatron is cultivated not only through the formal practice of meditation but through the daily act of turning inward, of listening to the whispers of intuition and honoring the insights that arise. In this way, meditation becomes a way of life, where each moment is infused with a sense of sacredness, a continuous alignment with the divine energy that flows within and around all things.

Ultimately, Metatron reveals that meditation is not merely a tool for peace or clarity but a bridge to the soul's deepest purpose. It is a path to spiritual communion, a journey that leads the seeker ever closer to the divine source, where the boundaries between self and spirit dissolve. In this unity, the seeker experiences the true essence of meditation—a state of being where the soul resonates in harmony with the universe, illuminated by Metatron's light, guided by wisdom, and filled with an abiding peace that transcends all understanding.

Chapter 6
Energy Cleansing

The journey of spiritual awakening calls for regular cleansing of the energy body—a ritual of purification that removes accumulated blockages, freeing the spirit to move forward unburdened and open to divine guidance. Archangel Metatron, with his radiant energy, acts as a beacon, leading the seeker through these cleansing practices. Just as physical spaces gather dust over time, so too does the spiritual body accumulate energies that can weigh down the spirit, cloud the mind, and disrupt the natural flow of vitality. Through Metatron's presence, the seeker learns that energy cleansing is not merely an occasional practice but a fundamental ritual that sustains spiritual health, creating a clear channel for higher awareness and peace.

The first step in energy cleansing is developing an awareness of the energies that surround and fill us. Metatron encourages the seeker to cultivate sensitivity to their energy field, noticing shifts in mood, thoughts, or physical sensations that may indicate an imbalance. These disturbances often signal areas where stagnant or negative energy has accumulated. By observing these signs, the seeker begins to understand their energy as a living entity, one that requires care and attention, much like the physical body.

One of the simplest yet powerful cleansing methods is the use of herbal baths, which utilize the natural properties of plants to purify the spirit. In this practice, Metatron's light is invoked as the seeker prepares a bath infused with cleansing herbs such as sage, lavender, or rosemary. These herbs carry grounding and protective qualities, each with its own unique vibration that harmonizes with the seeker's energy. As the seeker immerses in the bath, they visualize Metatron's energy flowing through the water, dissolving tension, and washing away energetic impurities. With each breath, a feeling of renewal emerges, as though layers of heaviness are lifted, leaving a sense of clarity and lightness.

Beyond herbal baths, Metatron guides the seeker in the practice of smudging—a ritual of smoke purification that has been used in various spiritual traditions to cleanse both spaces and individuals. Using sacred plants such as sage, palo santo, or cedar, the seeker lights the smudge stick and allows the smoke to rise, carrying away any stagnant or negative energy. In this ritual, Metatron's light is present, magnifying the smoke's power to cleanse. As the seeker waves the smoke around their body or their surroundings, they envision Metatron's light moving through the smoke, purifying their aura and creating a protective shield. This practice clears not only the energy body but also the spaces in which one lives, turning them into sanctuaries of peace and positive energy.

Another essential aspect of energy cleansing involves grounding exercises, which help reconnect the seeker to the earth, releasing excess or unwanted energy. Metatron guides the seeker to a quiet place outdoors, where they can sit or stand on the earth. The seeker is encouraged to close their eyes, feeling the earth's support beneath them, and to visualize roots extending from the base of their spine or their feet, deep into the ground. Metatron's energy moves with these roots, guiding any stagnant energy down into the earth, where it is absorbed and transformed. This grounding practice stabilizes the energy field, providing a sense of security and calm that reinforces the seeker's connection to both the physical and spiritual realms.

To enhance the energy cleansing process, Metatron introduces the seeker to the use of visualizations involving his sacred geometric light. By imagining Metatron's Cube surrounding the body, the seeker creates a powerful field of purifying energy. This geometric form, with its interconnected lines and points, represents divine order and acts as a filter, attracting and neutralizing negative energies within the aura. As the seeker envisions the Cube rotating around them, any remaining impurities dissolve, replaced by a feeling of balance and wholeness. This visualization is not only a method of cleansing but a reminder of the seeker's connection to divine harmony, aligning their energy with universal truth.

In moments of intense stress or emotional heaviness, Metatron encourages the use of breathwork as an immediate and accessible tool for energy cleansing. The seeker takes deep, intentional breaths, inhaling clarity and exhaling any burdens or negativity. With each breath, Metatron's light enters, infusing every cell with peace, while the exhale releases tension and anxiety. This rhythmic breathing not only cleanses but restores the flow of energy, creating a sense of renewal that grounds the seeker in the present. By focusing solely on the breath and Metatron's light, the seeker finds a quick and effective way to realign their energy in moments of need.

These cleansing practices extend beyond personal energy; they influence the way the seeker interacts with the world. Through regular energy cleansing, the seeker becomes a vessel of positive, clear energy, contributing to the upliftment of their surroundings. As they move through spaces and engage with others, their cleansed energy naturally creates an aura of peace, affecting all they encounter. Metatron reminds the seeker that energy is contagious, and by maintaining a state of purity, they serve as a beacon of light, subtly guiding others toward harmony and clarity.

In this process, Metatron's guidance emphasizes that energy cleansing is an act of self-love and respect. It is a ritual that honors the spiritual journey, ensuring that the energy body remains as clear as the intentions and aspirations within. By dedicating time to these cleansing practices, the seeker demonstrates a commitment to their spiritual well-being, creating a strong foundation for the deeper explorations to come. Each act of cleansing, whether a simple breath or a full ritual, renews the bond with Metatron, reinforcing the connection that sustains the seeker on the path of spiritual awakening.

Through this dedication, the seeker begins to experience life in a state of clarity and openness, a readiness to receive guidance and insight without the interference of unresolved energies. In this purified state, the energy body becomes a clear channel, where the divine can flow freely, enriching each moment with purpose and peace. Metatron's light, ever-present in these practices, serves as a reminder that energy is sacred, and by caring for it, the seeker honors the divine essence within.

As the seeker delves deeper into the art of energy cleansing, Archangel Metatron guides them toward more advanced techniques that refine and strengthen the spiritual body. These practices go beyond basic purification, incorporating methods that protect, empower, and align the energy centers, creating a foundation for sustained spiritual growth. Under Metatron's presence, the cleansing process becomes a transformative ritual, one that not only purifies but also fortifies, ensuring that each chakra resonates with a clarity and strength that supports the seeker's highest purpose.

At the heart of these advanced cleansing practices is the concept of energy alignment after purification. When cleansing the energy body, one removes impurities, but it is alignment that creates a balanced flow, grounding and stabilizing the energy field. Metatron's presence assists the seeker in visualizing each chakra as a vibrant, spinning wheel of light, each color aligned with its unique frequency. Beginning at the root and moving upward to the crown, the seeker imagines Metatron's light touching each chakra, harmonizing it, and releasing any lingering tension. This alignment practice, done after cleansing, ensures that energy flows evenly, creating a feeling of centeredness and unity within.

One profound method Metatron introduces is the ritual of energizing crystals for each chakra. Crystals are natural amplifiers, each with a vibration that resonates uniquely with different energy centers. By charging crystals with Metatron's energy, the seeker enhances their ability to cleanse and align the chakras. For instance, red jasper for the root chakra, carnelian for the sacral, and citrine for the solar plexus amplify the energy of these foundational centers. Amethyst at the crown and lapis lazuli at the third eye deepen spiritual insight. The seeker holds each crystal, visualizing Metatron's light merging with its energy, and places it over the corresponding chakra. This ritual not only cleanses but reinforces each chakra's strength, anchoring it with a clear and steady vibration.

Metatron further teaches the seeker the use of protection and energizing rituals to guard against external influences. Energetic protection is essential for maintaining the clarity achieved through cleansing, as external energies from interactions, environments, or even thoughts can disrupt the balance. Metatron guides the seeker in creating an energetic shield, visualizing a sphere of light surrounding the body. This sphere, infused with Metatron's presence, acts as a filter, allowing positive energies to enter while blocking or neutralizing negativity. In this protected space, the seeker feels secure, empowered to move through the world with a clear and resilient energy field.

In addition to crystal and protection rituals, Metatron introduces the seeker to advanced visualization techniques that work on a cellular level. By envisioning each cell in the body as a small, radiant point of light, the seeker directs Metatron's energy inward, filling every part of the physical form with a pure, vibrant glow. This visualization reinforces the connection between body and spirit, creating a sense of wholeness and alignment that extends beyond the chakras into the deepest layers of the self. Each cell vibrates with Metatron's light, creating a state of energetic harmony that renews the body's strength, resilience, and spiritual openness.

Metatron also emphasizes the importance of daily maintenance rituals for energy stability. These rituals, though brief, reinforce the cleansing work and maintain high vibration throughout the day. The seeker may start each morning with a simple breathing exercise, visualizing Metatron's light entering with each inhale and releasing stagnant energy with each exhale. During the day, the seeker can perform quick grounding exercises, such as touching the earth, or pausing to reconnect with the breath. These small, intentional practices act as reminders, keeping the energy body clear and resilient in the face of daily challenges.

For deeper cleansing, Metatron introduces the practice of chakra-focused sound cleansing. Sound, as a vibrational tool, can penetrate and purify each chakra, dissolving blockages with its resonant frequencies. The seeker may use singing bowls, tuning forks, or even vocal toning to create sounds that resonate with each chakra. Metatron's energy is visualized flowing through these sounds, amplifying their cleansing effect. As the sound vibrates through each chakra, it releases stagnant energy, leaving behind a state of purity and harmony. This practice not only clears but energizes, leaving each chakra fully activated and balanced, ready to support the seeker's spiritual journey.

Metatron's guidance also extends to the use of his sacred geometric forms, particularly Metatron's Cube, as a powerful cleansing tool. The seeker visualizes the Cube rotating around the body, spinning with a vibrant energy that clears blockages and restores balance. As the Cube rotates, it gathers and releases negative energy, replacing it with a field of pure, radiant light. This geometric energy creates a sense of harmony within the seeker's aura, a perfect alignment of energy that strengthens the connection to the divine. By regularly working with Metatron's Cube, the seeker experiences a profound state of energetic integrity, where each aspect of their being resonates in unity.

Metatron emphasizes the importance of closing each cleansing ritual with gratitude and intention setting. Gratitude acknowledges the divine support present in the cleansing process, grounding the seeker in humility and awareness. By expressing thanks to Metatron, the seeker reinforces the connection to this guiding energy, opening themselves to continued support and insight. Setting an intention, such as protection, peace, or clarity, helps anchor the effects of the cleansing ritual, creating a focused energy that resonates throughout the day.

Through these advanced cleansing practices, the seeker develops a refined understanding of their energy field, one that goes beyond purification to encompass protection, alignment, and empowerment. Metatron's teachings reveal that energy cleansing is a dynamic, ongoing process—a ritual of devotion that nurtures the spiritual body and maintains a state of openness to divine guidance. In this state of energetic clarity, the seeker experiences life as a flow of harmonious interactions, each moment a chance to embody the purity and balance achieved through these practices.

With Metatron's light as a constant guide, the seeker learns to move through life with an aura of peace and resilience. The energy body, purified and aligned, becomes a channel for divine wisdom, a vessel capable of receiving and radiating the light of the higher self. Each ritual strengthens this channel, creating a state of unity within, where the seeker feels deeply connected to both the self and the universe. Through this journey of energy cleansing, the seeker steps into a life of spiritual clarity, a path illuminated by Metatron's light, where the soul resonates in harmony with the rhythm of the cosmos.

Chapter 7
Spiritual Protection

As the seeker progresses on the path of spiritual development, a profound need for spiritual protection becomes clear. While spiritual growth opens new realms of understanding and connection, it also makes the energy body more sensitive to external influences. Here, Archangel Metatron steps forward as a vigilant protector, guiding the seeker in building a shield of light around their energy field. Spiritual protection, under Metatron's guidance, is not about isolation from the world but about cultivating strength and resilience, enabling the seeker to move through life with openness and peace, unaffected by negativity or discordant energies.

The foundation of spiritual protection begins with the creation of an energetic shield—a personal field of light that deflects negative influences while allowing positive energies to flow freely. Metatron guides the seeker through this process, encouraging visualization as a powerful tool for protection. The seeker is invited to sit in a quiet, focused state, visualizing a sphere of radiant light surrounding their entire body. This light may take on hues of white, gold, or violet, colors that resonate with high vibrations and purity. With Metatron's presence, this sphere becomes a living shield, pulsating with strength, attuned to the seeker's intention for peace, safety, and clarity.

The next step involves programming the shield to respond to various energies encountered in daily life. Metatron instructs the seeker to set clear intentions for this protective field, mentally affirming its purpose: to allow only energies of love, truth, and light to enter, while gently repelling those that carry discord, fear, or resentment. In this way, the shield is not rigid but intelligent, able to discern between energies that nourish and those that disrupt. This practice gives the seeker autonomy over their energy space, creating a layer of awareness and control that is empowering, yet aligned with a sense of compassion and openness.

In addition to visualizing a protective shield, Metatron introduces the seeker to grounding techniques that root this protection in the physical world. Grounding serves as a bridge between the spiritual and physical realms, reinforcing the seeker's connection to the earth and enhancing the stability of their protective field. One grounding method involves standing barefoot on natural ground, allowing the feet to sink slightly into the earth, and visualizing roots extending from the soles, deep into the soil. Metatron's energy flows down these roots, linking the seeker's aura to the strength and stability of the earth. This grounding practice anchors the shield in a solid foundation, ensuring that the seeker's energy remains steady and resilient, regardless of external fluctuations.

Metatron's role as a guardian also extends to teaching techniques for identifying and understanding energetic boundaries. Boundaries are an essential part of spiritual protection, defining the space where one's energy begins and ends. Through his guidance, the seeker learns to sense their energetic boundaries by becoming aware of subtle shifts in mood, sensation, or thought patterns when interacting with others or entering different environments. With time and practice, these boundaries become more pronounced, allowing the seeker to detect when their energy field is being affected by external influences. In moments where a boundary feels compromised, Metatron's light can be called upon, reinforcing the seeker's aura and creating a renewed sense of security.

To further strengthen spiritual protection, Metatron introduces the seeker to the art of invoking his presence as a guardian of the energy field. This invocation is simple yet profound, a request for Metatron's support and vigilance. The seeker is encouraged to set aside a moment each morning to invite Metatron's light to envelop their energy field, visualizing him as a powerful guardian who stands watch. This daily invocation serves as a reminder of Metatron's protective energy, fostering a sense of companionship and support on the spiritual path. With each invocation, the seeker strengthens their connection to Metatron, developing an inner trust in his presence as a constant source of protection.

As the seeker grows more adept in maintaining their shield, Metatron introduces them to techniques for reinforcing it in challenging situations. One such technique is the "armor of light" visualization, where the seeker imagines a layer of shimmering light covering their body, almost like a suit of armor, flexible yet impenetrable. This armor protects without restricting, providing a layer of defense that deflects negative influences. Metatron's light moves through this armor, empowering it with resilience, allowing the seeker to navigate difficult interactions or environments with calm and assurance.

In moments of heightened vulnerability—such as times of stress, fatigue, or emotional turbulence—Metatron advises additional practices for fortifying the shield. These moments may leave the seeker's energy more susceptible to external influences, and Metatron suggests grounding exercises, deep breaths, or even a quick visualization of a protective sphere of light. These brief but intentional actions restore the integrity of the shield, allowing the seeker to return to a state of balance and protection quickly.

Spiritual protection, as Metatron reveals, is not merely a defensive measure; it is also a way of preserving the sacred space within. This protection supports the seeker's openness to divine guidance, allowing Metatron's wisdom to flow freely without interference. As the shield becomes a natural extension of the seeker's energy, it fosters a sense of inner sanctity—a recognition that the energy field is a vessel for the soul, deserving of respect and care. Through this practice, the seeker learns to walk through life with a quiet confidence, aware of their own strength and secure in the knowledge that their energy is safeguarded.

Metatron teaches that true spiritual protection is a balance between openness and strength, where the seeker remains receptive to the light and beauty of the world without absorbing its discordant elements. This awareness of protection deepens the seeker's ability to connect with others compassionately, without losing their own center. It allows them to navigate the spiritual path with a clear focus, unencumbered by energies that would pull them off course. The journey becomes one of purpose and clarity, guided by Metatron's protective presence, a light that shields as it guides.

Here, the seeker discovers that spiritual protection is a skill, a practice, and a state of being. Through Metatron's teachings, they embrace this protection not as a barrier but as an enhancement to their own energy, a sacred boundary that honors the self and the spiritual journey. This balance of strength and compassion allows the seeker to engage deeply with the world, carrying Metatron's light as both a guardian and a guide, ensuring that the path ahead remains clear, safe, and illuminated.

As the seeker progresses in the practice of spiritual protection, Archangel Metatron reveals deeper techniques for maintaining and fortifying this sacred shield, enabling it to adapt to life's diverse situations. Spiritual protection is not merely a static defense but a living, dynamic practice that changes in response to the environment, the people, and the energies encountered. Through Metatron's teachings, the seeker learns how to nurture this protective field as an active, resilient energy, forming a barrier that not only guards but empowers them to move through the world with confidence and spiritual clarity.

Metatron begins by guiding the seeker in creating a ritual for daily renewal of the protective shield. This morning practice, simple yet profound, sets a powerful intention for the day, aligning the seeker's energy with protection and balance. Seated quietly, the seeker visualizes a sphere of radiant light surrounding their body, filling the aura with a warm and impenetrable glow.

As Metatron's energy flows into this light, the sphere expands, creating a field of gentle, steady protection. The seeker is encouraged to affirm aloud or within, "I am shielded in divine light, guarded by Metatron's strength." This affirmation, infused with intent, strengthens the shield and aligns it with Metatron's presence, establishing a foundation of security that extends throughout the day.

In addition to a morning ritual, Metatron teaches specific techniques to reinforce the shield in moments of vulnerability. When the seeker encounters intense energies—whether in busy environments, emotionally charged interactions, or situations of conflict—the shield can be instantly re-strengthened by visualizing Metatron's Cube. This sacred geometric symbol is imagined rotating slowly around the body, emanating a luminous energy that absorbs negativity and fortifies the seeker's aura. As the Cube spins, each line and angle of light creates a layer of protection, forming a complex but seamless shield that leaves the seeker feeling calm, resilient, and untouched by external influences. This quick reinforcement can be performed discreetly in any situation, providing an immediate barrier of protection when needed.

Metatron also introduces the seeker to a practice for cleansing and renewing the shield at the end of each day. Through this ritual, the seeker releases any energies they may have absorbed, restoring the purity of their protective field. To begin, Metatron's presence is invited to surround the seeker, who visualizes a soft, violet light descending from above, cleansing the aura from head to toe. As this light washes over the shield, it dissolves any lingering influences, emotional residues, or psychic attachments, leaving the field clear and renewed. This cleansing light reinforces the protective shield, transforming it into a space of quiet rest and resilience, a sanctuary for the spirit that is both protected and refreshed.

Beyond rituals, Metatron introduces specific physical practices that enhance protection in everyday life, including grounding exercises and the use of specific crystals. Grounding is essential for maintaining a strong, stable aura; Metatron encourages the seeker to connect with the earth by spending time in nature, touching the ground, or walking barefoot. This physical connection to the earth provides a counterbalance to the spiritual protection, anchoring the seeker's energy and reinforcing the shield from a place of calm and stability. Similarly, crystals such as black tourmaline, obsidian, or smoky quartz can be carried as personal talismans. These stones are renowned for their grounding and protective qualities, absorbing negative energies while enhancing the strength of the aura. When used with Metatron's guidance, these crystals become an extension of the seeker's energy, harmonizing with the shield and amplifying its effect.

To maintain this dynamic protection, Metatron also teaches techniques for detecting subtle shifts in the shield, enabling the seeker to become sensitive to any changes in their protective field. Through mindful self-awareness, the seeker begins to sense when the shield weakens or becomes thin, often through a subtle feeling of discomfort, tiredness, or heightened sensitivity to others' emotions. In these moments, Metatron's presence is called upon, immediately replenishing the field with a renewed layer of strength. The seeker learns to see this awareness as an act of self-respect, a dedication to maintaining the integrity of their spiritual journey. Each recalibration of the shield becomes a moment of honoring the sacred boundary between self and world.

Another profound aspect of Metatron's teachings on protection is the power of setting boundaries. Boundaries, though invisible, are the pillars of spiritual protection, defining where the seeker's energy ends and external energy begins. Metatron guides the seeker in clarifying these boundaries, learning to say "no" when necessary, and preserving the sanctity of their energy space. Through practices of discernment, the seeker becomes adept at recognizing situations, relationships, and environments that align or clash with their vibrational state. This discernment is not about judgment but awareness, a compassionate respect for both the self and others. Metatron's teachings reveal that boundaries are expressions of inner strength, allowing the seeker to engage deeply with the world without sacrificing personal energy or spiritual clarity.

In times of deep need or when faced with particularly challenging energies, Metatron offers a ritual of invoking archangelic guardianship, surrounding the seeker with additional protection. By calling on Metatron and inviting his presence as a guardian, the seeker visualizes multiple layers of light, each imbued with Metatron's strength and compassion. These layers form a protective shield of multi-faceted light, each one a barrier that filters out negativity and reinforces the seeker's resilience. This practice is especially powerful during times of transition, travel, or personal upheaval, creating a space where the seeker feels completely held and safeguarded, able to stand firmly in their spiritual truth.

Ultimately, Metatron's teachings on spiritual protection reveal that it is not an isolated practice but a way of life. Protection, as Metatron imparts, is the cultivation of a harmonious energy field, a balanced aura that moves through the world without being influenced by external turmoil. This shield of light is not a barrier of isolation, but an invitation to engage with life from a place of inner peace. With each layer of protection established, the seeker gains the freedom to grow, learn, and expand in alignment with their higher purpose, supported by Metatron's unwavering presence.

Through these practices, the seeker embodies a state of quiet power, a gentle but unbreakable resilience that radiates from within. Metatron's light becomes a constant force that not only protects but inspires, guiding the seeker to live with integrity and courage. In this state, spiritual protection is transformed from a need into an essence—a continuous, sacred alignment that honors the seeker's unique path. The seeker moves forward with Metatron's light as both shield and guide, grounded in purpose, protected in spirit, and ready to embrace the world with an open, steady heart.

Chapter 8
Expansion of Consciousness

As the seeker's journey deepens, the time arrives to transcend the familiar boundaries of perception and begin exploring the vast expanses of consciousness. Guided by Archangel Metatron, this expansion is not a leap into the unknown but a deliberate opening of awareness—a soft, steady unveiling of the soul's infinite potential. Metatron, who stands at the intersection of earthly and divine wisdom, becomes the ultimate guide, encouraging the seeker to explore new dimensions of insight, intuition, and understanding. Here, the concept of consciousness is not merely an abstract state but a living, breathing reality, one that reveals life's mysteries and the interconnectedness of all beings.

Metatron introduces the seeker to the foundations of expanded consciousness, beginning with the cultivation of inner stillness. In a world filled with endless stimuli and distractions, the first step toward conscious expansion is the creation of silence within. Through Metatron's guidance, the seeker practices quieting the mind, allowing thoughts to settle like particles in a still lake. In this state of calm, subtle intuitions begin to surface—whispers from the soul that reveal insights beyond logic. Metatron's presence intensifies this silence, creating a sanctuary of peace where awareness blooms naturally, free from the interference of everyday concerns.

With this inner stillness established, Metatron leads the seeker into practices that awaken the mind to higher perceptions. Visualization is one of the primary tools, a way of accessing dimensions that lie beyond ordinary sight. Metatron guides the seeker to visualize an open sky within the mind's eye—a vast, limitless expanse, filled with light. In this sky, each thought, emotion, and sensation appears as a cloud, moving across but never defining the sky itself. By observing these clouds without attachment, the seeker begins to understand consciousness as the pure space behind thoughts, the quiet awareness that exists independently of mental activity. This practice expands the seeker's sense of identity, shifting from the surface of thought to the vastness of conscious presence.

Metatron then introduces a powerful exercise known as "the heart of the universe." Here, the seeker is guided to focus on the heart center, visualizing it as a portal that opens to universal consciousness. As Metatron's light fills the heart, it expands, reaching beyond the individual self and connecting with the energetic field that flows through all beings. In this state, the seeker senses the pulse of life itself—a rhythm that unites every soul, every creature, every element in the cosmos. This exercise is a profound experience of unity, a reminder that consciousness is not contained within one mind but is a shared essence that transcends all separation.

To deepen this connection, Metatron introduces practices for awakening intuition, an essential aspect of expanded consciousness. Intuition, as Metatron teaches, is the soul's language—a way of receiving wisdom that does not rely on logic but on a direct, inner knowing. The seeker is guided to trust the quiet nudges and impressions that arise during moments of reflection, learning to distinguish the voice of intuition from the noise of the mind. By asking questions in meditation and then releasing them to Metatron's guidance, the seeker often finds answers emerging organically, as though from a deeper source of truth. These insights reveal a consciousness that moves beyond personal experience, tapping into a universal intelligence that holds knowledge timeless and profound.

As the seeker's intuition strengthens, Metatron encourages the development of symbolic perception—the ability to see meaning in everyday experiences. In expanded consciousness, life itself becomes a language, where each encounter, symbol, and event carries guidance. A feather on the path, a recurring number, or a chance meeting are no longer seen as random; instead, they are recognized as messages from the universe, signs that reveal deeper truths and encourage alignment with the soul's purpose. Through Metatron's guidance, the seeker learns to interpret these symbols intuitively, developing an awareness that allows for continuous dialogue with the divine.

Metatron also reveals the importance of maintaining balance in this expansion, reminding the seeker that true growth respects the harmony between earthly grounding and spiritual insight. Practices of grounding, such as mindful walking or connecting with nature, are essential companions to conscious expansion. These grounding practices allow the seeker to remain rooted in the present, integrating the insights gained from higher consciousness into daily life. Metatron's energy acts as an anchor, a steady presence that prevents the seeker from becoming overwhelmed by the vastness of expanded awareness. This balance ensures that spiritual growth enhances, rather than disrupts, the seeker's experience of life.

In moments of heightened awareness, the seeker may feel a profound shift in perception, where the boundaries between self and world blur. Metatron teaches the seeker to navigate these states of oneness with openness and humility, encouraging them to embrace the interconnectedness of all things without losing the sense of self. In these moments, the world is perceived not as a series of separate entities but as an expression of one consciousness, a web of life woven together by threads of shared existence. Through this awareness, the seeker's perspective transforms, moving from personal concerns to a broader, more inclusive understanding of reality.

Through each of these practices, Metatron reveals that expanded consciousness is not an escape from the world but a deeper engagement with it. As the seeker awakens to higher states of awareness, life becomes a continuous, flowing meditation, where each thought, action, and interaction is infused with a sense of sacredness. The expanded consciousness allows for a view of life that is both vast and intimate, a space where the soul feels at home within the cosmos. Metatron's teachings provide not only the tools for this journey but also the strength to embrace the unknown, to trust in the divine order, and to step into the mystery with confidence and grace.

Here, the seeker begins to see consciousness as a boundless field, one that invites exploration but requires respect, patience, and guidance. Metatron's presence serves as both a guide and a protector, leading the seeker deeper into this state of unity while ensuring they remain connected to their own essence. With each step, the seeker feels Metatron's light within and around, a reminder that the journey into expanded consciousness is a return to the self, a rediscovery of the truth that lies at the core of all existence. Through this expansion, the seeker touches the eternal, awakening to a life filled with purpose, wonder, and an abiding peace that transcends the boundaries of the ordinary world.

As the seeker journeys further into the expansion of consciousness, Archangel Metatron offers practices that deepen this awakening, unveiling realms of wisdom and intuition that guide one to profound spiritual understanding. In this heightened state, consciousness begins to transcend everyday awareness, allowing the seeker to access layers of intuition and inner knowing that reflect the truth of the higher self. This journey into expanded consciousness is not merely about acquiring knowledge but about experiencing a profound connection with the divine, with life, and with the vastness within.

With Metatron's guidance, the seeker begins by developing practices for refining their intuitive abilities. Intuition, as Metatron teaches, is not a gift given to a few but a natural aspect of consciousness available to all who seek it. To access this intuitive wisdom, the seeker must quiet the mind and open the heart, creating a space where insights can arise freely. Metatron introduces a method known as "the inner sanctuary," a practice where the seeker visualizes a sacred, tranquil place within, untouched by the distractions of the outer world. In this sanctuary, the seeker poses questions or reflects on decisions, trusting in the intuitive responses that emerge, often as subtle impressions or gentle nudges. With practice, this connection with intuition strengthens, becoming a trusted inner guide that offers wisdom aligned with the seeker's highest path.

Another essential practice Metatron imparts is the opening of "spiritual vision," or the ability to perceive energies and truths beyond the physical. This practice involves the activation of the third eye, the chakra associated with inner vision, clarity, and insight. Metatron guides the seeker in focusing on this center, visualizing it as an indigo light radiating from the forehead. As the seeker breathes into this space, Metatron's energy flows into the third eye, awakening its perception and deepening the ability to see beyond appearances. In time, this practice reveals a more profound vision of the world, where the seeker perceives the energetic layers that connect all beings, as well as the subtle threads of intention, emotion, and purpose that shape each interaction.

In this state of expanded perception, Metatron introduces the seeker to the practice of seeing "spiritual symbols," messages that appear in the mind's eye or even in daily life as reflections of higher truths. These symbols may take the form of geometric shapes, colors, or scenes that resonate deeply, each carrying a unique message for the seeker's path. Metatron encourages the seeker to interpret these symbols intuitively, trusting that the meaning will reveal itself in due time. Over time, these symbols become personal guides, reminders of lessons, insights, or encouragements from the higher self. This practice builds a direct line of communication with the divine, allowing the seeker to receive guidance that transcends the limits of language or logic.

Metatron also leads the seeker into the practice of "cosmic attunement," where the seeker aligns their consciousness with the rhythms of the universe. By attuning to the cycles of nature, the phases of the moon, or the shifting seasons, the seeker learns to flow with universal energies rather than resist them. During meditative practice, the seeker visualizes their heart beating in rhythm with the pulse of the cosmos, feeling the unity between their inner world and the larger, cosmic dance of life. In this state, the seeker perceives time not as a series of isolated moments but as a continuous, interconnected flow. This awareness fosters a sense of harmony with the greater whole, a reminder that all existence moves together in cycles of creation, transformation, and renewal.

To deepen this attunement, Metatron introduces the practice of "spiritual alignment," where the seeker aligns their own consciousness with the energy of Metatron himself. This alignment involves visualizing Metatron's radiant light flowing down through the crown chakra, filling the entire being with a divine frequency. As this light moves through each chakra, it harmonizes the seeker's energy with Metatron's presence, creating a sense of unity and alignment that enhances clarity and intuition. In this state, the seeker experiences a resonance with Metatron's wisdom, an alignment that clears mental fog and opens a direct pathway to deeper understanding. This alignment practice strengthens the bond with Metatron, reinforcing his guidance as a constant source of support on the journey of expanded consciousness.

In this phase of expanded awareness, Metatron also emphasizes the importance of grounding the newfound insights into everyday life. Expanded consciousness, though transcendent, must be integrated into the world for its effects to fully unfold. Metatron introduces practices of "embodied awareness," where the seeker, after each meditative or intuitive experience, returns to the present moment, consciously integrating insights by performing simple acts with mindful attention. Whether through preparing a meal, speaking kindly to others, or attending to daily tasks, these moments of mindful action become channels through which higher consciousness manifests in the physical world, grounding the divine into the ordinary.

Metatron teaches that expanded consciousness is a continuous process, a path that requires patience, humility, and balance. He encourages the seeker to embrace moments of stillness and reflection, allowing time for each insight to settle and for the new awareness to become a natural part of their being. The seeker learns that true spiritual expansion is not marked by grand revelations alone but by subtle shifts in perception, a deepening sense of unity, and an abiding peace that permeates all aspects of life.

Through this journey, Metatron reveals that expanded consciousness brings with it an expanded capacity for compassion and love. As the seeker touches the interconnectedness of all things, an awareness of unity emerges, a profound empathy that recognizes the shared journey of every soul. This expanded consciousness fosters a love that is universal, extending beyond personal boundaries to embrace all of existence. Metatron teaches that this love is the essence of higher awareness, a force that guides every thought, word, and action toward the service of a greater good.

In these moments of unity and peace, the seeker experiences the true nature of expanded consciousness—a return to the soul's original harmony, a state of being that transcends separation. Metatron's presence illuminates this path, showing the seeker that expanded consciousness is not a final destination but a way of engaging with life itself. Through these practices, the seeker learns to navigate both the seen and unseen realms with wisdom, grace, and an open heart, living as a bridge between the physical and the divine, a vessel of love and truth.

With each practice, each moment of insight, the seeker discovers a deeper connection to the universe, a resonance that brings both peace and purpose. Through Metatron's guidance, expanded consciousness becomes a journey of remembering—a return to the wholeness and unity that lies within every soul, a journey where the divine is not a distant reality but a living presence within, guiding, loving, and forever illuminating the way.

Chapter 9
Positive Manifestation

As the seeker delves into the art of manifestation, Archangel Metatron guides them to understand that true manifestation is a process of aligning with the highest purpose and invoking the creative force of the universe. Manifestation, in its essence, is more than the act of drawing things into one's life; it is an intentional co-creation with the divine. With Metatron's support, the seeker learns that each thought, emotion, and intention carries a frequency, a vibration that attracts experiences, relationships, and opportunities resonating with that same energy. Positive manifestation, therefore, begins by cultivating a state of inner alignment, where desires are not only about personal gain but reflect a higher purpose.

Metatron teaches the seeker to begin with clarity of intention, a foundational step that shapes the entire manifestation process. The seeker is guided to reflect on what they truly wish to create, understanding that desires aligned with the soul's purpose flow effortlessly, while those born of ego or fleeting impulses often lead to stagnation. Metatron's light encourages the seeker to ask questions that delve into the essence of their desires: "Is this aligned with my growth? Does it serve a greater purpose?" This process of introspection not only refines the seeker's goals but connects them to a deeper source of meaning, ensuring that each intention is rooted in authenticity and spiritual alignment.

To further enhance clarity, Metatron introduces a visualization technique known as "the heart of desire." In this practice, the seeker visualizes their intention as a radiant light within the heart center, glowing with warmth and clarity. As they breathe into this light, it grows stronger, illuminating every aspect of the desire. This focused awareness brings out details and sensations, making the vision vivid and real. Metatron's presence infuses this light, encouraging the seeker to hold this image in a state of love and gratitude, aligning the heart and mind with the vision. Through this visualization, the intention becomes more than a thought; it transforms into a heartfelt frequency that resonates through the seeker's entire being.

With the intention clear and infused with love, Metatron guides the seeker to focus on aligning the energy centers, or chakras, with the desired manifestation. Each chakra plays a role in the manifestation process, creating a channel through which divine energy flows from vision to reality. Starting with the root chakra, Metatron encourages the seeker to feel grounded, connected to the earth, creating a stable foundation. Moving upward, the sacral chakra infuses creativity, the solar plexus empowers with determination, the heart brings compassion, the throat expresses truth, the third eye provides vision, and the crown opens to divine inspiration. As each chakra aligns, the intention becomes a full-bodied expression of the seeker's spiritual purpose, resonating with a frequency that attracts what is needed for manifestation.

Metatron also emphasizes the power of affirmations in positive manifestation, teaching the seeker to use words as carriers of intention. Words, when spoken or thought with purpose, send vibrational signals that shape one's reality. The seeker is guided to create affirmations that reflect their desires in the present tense, affirming the truth of the vision as if it already exists. Metatron's energy supports this process, amplifying the affirmations with divine light, turning them into mantras of manifestation. Repeating these affirmations daily, with faith and conviction, reinforces the belief in the desired reality, attracting energies and opportunities that align with the vision.

To deepen the practice, Metatron introduces the concept of "detachment," a state of surrender that allows the intention to manifest without clinging or resistance. Detachment does not mean indifference; rather, it is a trust in the universe, an understanding that the timing and form of the manifestation may unfold in ways the seeker cannot foresee. Metatron teaches that by releasing control, the seeker opens the path for divine alignment, allowing the universe to respond in its perfect timing. This detachment, coupled with gratitude, transforms the manifestation process into a partnership, where the seeker's faith in the divine replaces the need for constant validation.

Gratitude, as Metatron reveals, is a powerful force in manifestation, a frequency that magnifies intentions and accelerates their realization. By expressing gratitude for the desired outcome as if it has already arrived, the seeker enters a state of receptivity and abundance. This gratitude is not limited to moments of success; it becomes a daily practice, a way of acknowledging the beauty and support present in each step of the journey. Metatron encourages the seeker to cultivate this gratitude with a humble heart, recognizing each manifestation, big or small, as a gift that deepens the connection to the divine.

In times when manifestation seems slow or uncertain, Metatron offers guidance in maintaining a positive, elevated vibration, a state that aligns with higher energies and attracts opportunities aligned with the seeker's vision. This involves staying mindful of one's emotional and mental state, gently redirecting negative thoughts or doubts back to faith. Metatron's presence serves as a reminder that obstacles or delays are not setbacks but opportunities for growth, moments that refine the seeker's understanding and prepare them to receive the manifestation fully. Through this process, the seeker learns that positive manifestation is a journey of trust, patience, and surrender to divine wisdom.

Metatron encourages the seeker to view positive manifestation as a service, a way of bringing light into the world. When desires are aligned with compassion and generosity, they ripple outward, touching the lives of others in ways seen and unseen. By manifesting with a heart open to serve, the seeker becomes a conduit for divine energy, inviting the universe to work through them. Metatron's guidance reveals that each manifestation, when aligned with love, contributes to the collective well-being, creating harmony that extends beyond the individual.

Through these practices, positive manifestation is transformed from a wish into a sacred act of co-creation. Metatron's teachings guide the seeker in cultivating intentions that reflect the soul's purpose, in trusting the universe's timing, and in expressing gratitude for each step of the journey. The manifestation process becomes an inner alchemy, where desires are purified by love, intentions are aligned with divine flow, and each outcome is received as a blessing. In this state, the seeker discovers that true manifestation is not about control but about harmony, a dance with the universe that brings forth a life of purpose, fulfillment, and deep spiritual connection.

As the seeker continues to explore the art of positive manifestation, Archangel Metatron introduces deeper techniques that transform desires into realities with precision and spiritual alignment. These practices build on the foundation of intention and detachment, guiding the seeker to channel the power of visualizations and affirmations while embracing the subtle energies that connect all things. With Metatron's guidance, the seeker discovers that manifestation is not merely a linear process but an interwoven exchange with the universe—a process that invites surrender, focus, and an unshakable connection to the divine.

Metatron first emphasizes the practice of advanced visualization, an approach that deepens the seeker's connection to their intentions by engaging all senses. Through this immersive visualization, the seeker does not merely see their desired reality but experiences it in vivid detail. Metatron guides the seeker to close their eyes and step into this reality as if it is already present, feeling the textures, colors, and emotions that accompany this vision. The more tangible the visualization, the stronger the magnetic pull, drawing energies into alignment with the vision.

Metatron's presence enhances this experience, wrapping the vision in his light, amplifying its resonance with divine intention.

Another key technique Metatron introduces is the integration of chakras into the manifestation process, aligning each chakra's unique energy with the seeker's goals. Metatron teaches that each chakra holds specific qualities that can fuel manifestation—stability in the root chakra, creativity in the sacral, confidence in the solar plexus, love in the heart, truth in the throat, clarity in the third eye, and spiritual connection in the crown. Through a guided meditation, the seeker is encouraged to visualize their intention passing through each chakra, infusing the vision with the qualities of each energy center. As the intention moves through the chakras, it gains strength and dimension, becoming a balanced and complete desire rooted in all aspects of the self.

In this alignment, Metatron introduces the seeker to the power of vibrational resonance through mantras and sound. Sound, as a vibrational force, amplifies intentions and infuses them with energy that extends beyond the mind. Metatron guides the seeker to choose specific mantras that resonate with their intention—words or sounds that vibrate with positivity and purpose. By chanting these mantras regularly, the seeker creates a field of resonance that attracts experiences and opportunities aligned with the desired outcome. Metatron's energy joins this practice, intensifying the frequency, allowing the sound to travel deeper into the universe and drawing the manifestation closer with each repetition.

Metatron also offers guidance on practicing manifestation in harmony with lunar cycles, aligning with the natural rhythms of creation. The phases of the moon symbolize different stages of growth and release, and Metatron teaches the seeker how to synchronize intentions with these energies. During the new moon, the seeker plants seeds of intention, focusing on new beginnings. The waxing phase, which follows, is a time of building and nurturing the vision, while the full moon amplifies intentions, illuminating any adjustments needed to stay aligned. As the moon wanes, the seeker releases attachments and trusts in the unfolding. This harmony with lunar rhythms deepens the seeker's connection with the natural world, enhancing the manifestation process by aligning it with the cycles of life.

To strengthen the bond between the seeker's vision and the universe, Metatron introduces the concept of sacred symbols and sigils—visual representations of intentions crafted with focused intention. Metatron guides the seeker to draw or visualize a unique symbol that embodies their specific goal, allowing it to become a personal emblem of the desired reality. This symbol, when infused with Metatron's energy, acts as a beacon, sending a clear and concentrated message to the universe. The seeker can meditate on this symbol, place it on an altar, or carry it as a reminder of their goal. Over time, this symbol becomes a potent link to the intended outcome, a tangible focal point that channels the seeker's energy and amplifies the resonance of the manifestation.

Metatron also reveals the significance of daily gratitude as a practice that accelerates manifestation. Gratitude elevates vibration and reinforces a state of receptivity, inviting abundance. The seeker is encouraged to express gratitude not only for present blessings but for the desired outcome, as if it has already manifested. By thanking the universe in advance, the seeker bridges the gap between desire and reality, creating a space where manifestation flows effortlessly. This gratitude, rooted in faith, strengthens the belief that all things are possible, aligning the seeker's energy with the natural abundance of the universe.

Another technique Metatron introduces is releasing limitations—beliefs or inner dialogues that may unknowingly hinder manifestation. The seeker is encouraged to examine any thoughts that cast doubt or impose limitations on their vision, observing these beliefs with compassion and detachment. Metatron guides the seeker in transforming limiting thoughts by replacing them with affirmations of possibility, trust, and openness. With each shift in belief, the seeker dissolves the barriers that may have held back their manifestations, creating an unencumbered channel for divine flow.

In moments when the manifestation journey becomes challenging or patience wears thin, Metatron teaches the seeker to turn inward, reconnecting with the core of faith and inner peace. In these times, Metatron's presence serves as a stabilizing force, a reminder that divine timing unfolds with perfect wisdom. The seeker learns that delays are often moments of alignment, where the universe orchestrates circumstances to bring forth the manifestation in its most harmonious form. By trusting in this timing, the seeker releases the need to control outcomes, allowing the process to flow naturally and peacefully, secure in the knowledge that each step is guided.

Through these practices, the seeker realizes that manifestation is more than an act of personal will; it is a dance with universal forces, a harmonious blend of intention, trust, and divine alignment. Metatron's guidance transforms the process into a sacred practice, a journey where each thought, action, and feeling becomes an offering to the universe. As the seeker's intentions unfold, they come to understand that each manifestation is a reflection of their inner growth, an expression of alignment with the divine path that Metatron illuminates.

In this realization, positive manifestation transcends mere desire—it becomes a celebration of spiritual connection, a testament to the seeker's evolving awareness and unity with all that is. The seeker, guided by Metatron, steps into their role as a conscious co-creator, a vessel for divine intention, manifesting a life of purpose, love, and fulfillment. Through this process, they embody the truth that each creation is both a journey inward and an offering outward, harmonizing the self with the infinite creative energy of the universe.

Chapter 10
Life Purpose

The journey of spiritual awakening is incomplete without exploring the profound question of life purpose. Archangel Metatron, as the seeker's guide, reveals that life purpose is not a single, static goal but an evolving expression of the soul's deepest calling. As the seeker learns to move beyond the roles, labels, and expectations imposed by the world, they begin to uncover the essence of who they truly are and the unique path they are meant to walk. Life purpose, in this context, is an alignment with one's highest self—a state in which actions, thoughts, and intentions reflect the soul's truth and contribute to a greater whole.

Metatron begins by encouraging the seeker to cultivate a state of quiet reflection, an inner stillness that allows them to listen to the whispers of the soul. In these moments of introspection, the seeker may begin to sense glimpses of purpose, felt as subtle inclinations or longings that resonate deeply within. Metatron's energy surrounds these reflections, helping the seeker to trust these inner prompts, to discern which impulses arise from their authentic self and which are merely reflections of external expectations. By tuning into this inner knowing, the seeker begins to distinguish the direction that aligns with their true purpose from paths that would lead them away from it.

One of the first practices Metatron introduces in the search for life purpose is the exploration of personal passions and natural talents. These passions—those activities or pursuits that bring a sense of joy, fulfillment, and timelessness—often serve as windows into the soul's calling. Metatron guides the seeker to create a space for these interests, no matter how modest, encouraging them to explore and nourish these parts of themselves. Each talent or passion, Metatron reveals, carries with it an energy, a frequency that resonates with the soul's journey. By honoring these interests, the seeker begins to cultivate an energy of authenticity and enthusiasm, qualities that are essential for manifesting purpose.

As the seeker connects with these talents and passions, Metatron invites them to reflect on moments of service, times when they felt a natural inclination to help, teach, or contribute to the well-being of others. Service, Metatron teaches, is often intertwined with life purpose, for purpose grows most fully in acts that extend beyond the self. In moments of helping others, the seeker may experience a heightened sense of connection, joy, or peace—signs that they are moving closer to their soul's path. Metatron's light illuminates these experiences, encouraging the seeker to reflect on how their unique abilities can serve the greater good, transforming individual gifts into acts of love and contribution.

To deepen this journey of discovery, Metatron guides the seeker in the practice of visualization, inviting them to imagine a life aligned fully with purpose. The seeker is encouraged to picture themselves living each day with a sense of fulfillment, engaging in activities that inspire joy and meaning. In this vision, they observe themselves interacting with others, contributing to the world, and growing spiritually. As Metatron infuses this vision with his energy, the seeker feels a sense of clarity, as though they are catching a glimpse of the path they are meant to walk. This visualization becomes a beacon, a reminder of the harmony that comes from living in alignment with purpose.

Metatron also teaches the seeker about the role of intuition in finding and following life purpose. Intuition, as the quiet voice of the soul, offers guidance that transcends logic, revealing paths that may initially seem unfamiliar or unexpected. Through Metatron's encouragement, the seeker learns to honor these intuitive insights, trusting that each nudge or feeling of resonance is a step toward a deeper truth. Whether it is a strong feeling to pursue a new skill, meet a person, or embark on an unfamiliar journey, these intuitive prompts are treated as sacred signposts, guiding the seeker closer to their unique purpose. With practice, the seeker's intuition strengthens, creating a compass that aligns with the soul's calling.

A pivotal part of discovering life purpose, as Metatron reveals, is embracing both strengths and challenges. The seeker is encouraged to reflect not only on their talents but also on their struggles, for these challenges often hold hidden lessons and unique insights. Metatron's presence brings a sense of acceptance, helping the seeker to view difficulties not as obstacles but as integral parts of the journey that shape and refine their purpose. Each challenge, each period of growth, deepens the seeker's understanding, revealing qualities of resilience, empathy, or wisdom that contribute to their mission. This acceptance of all aspects of oneself, strengths and shadows alike, fosters a sense of wholeness that is essential to living purposefully.

Metatron guides the seeker in developing a daily practice of intention-setting, a ritual that anchors their journey with purpose. Each morning, the seeker is encouraged to set an intention that reflects their desire to live with authenticity, compassion, and service. This intention becomes a seed planted in the heart, a subtle reminder to act in alignment with the soul's values. Metatron's energy strengthens this practice, transforming each intention into a vibrational field that shapes the day, attracting opportunities, connections, and experiences that align with purpose. Over time, these intentions help the seeker build a life that reflects their highest self, a life of coherence and inner peace.

In moments of uncertainty, Metatron reassures the seeker, reminding them that life purpose is not a destination but an evolving journey. Purpose can shift and expand over time, reflecting the growth and changes within the soul. Metatron teaches the seeker to remain open, to embrace flexibility, and to release attachment to a fixed outcome. This openness allows the seeker to flow with life's changes, discovering new layers of purpose as they deepen their relationship with themselves and the divine. Through this process, they come to understand that purpose is not bound to a specific role or achievement but is an ever-unfolding expression of the soul's essence.

Metatron's guidance illuminates the path of life purpose, not as a rigid plan but as a living, breathing journey of exploration and growth. Through quiet reflection, nurturing of talents, acts of service, and trust in intuition, the seeker draws closer to a life that resonates with their true calling. With each step, they feel a deeper sense of connection to the world, a sense that their actions contribute to something greater. This alignment with purpose brings a sense of peace, joy, and fulfillment, a knowing that each moment, each decision, is a part of the soul's sacred dance with the universe.

As the seeker moves further into understanding life purpose, Archangel Metatron offers advanced practices to deepen this connection, showing that living purposefully is not only about self-discovery but about harmonizing every aspect of life with the soul's true path. In this part of the journey, Metatron guides the seeker to explore purpose as a dynamic force, one that permeates thoughts, actions, and relationships, fostering a life that vibrates with alignment and fulfillment. Purpose is no longer viewed as a distant goal but as an ever-present state of being, continuously unfolding and growing as the seeker moves forward.

Metatron begins by guiding the seeker through a process of integrating purpose into daily actions, turning even the smallest choices into expressions of their soul's calling. To achieve this, the seeker learns to approach each day with mindfulness, setting a quiet intention each morning to align their actions with their deeper values. In this practice, the seeker connects with Metatron, who encourages them to approach each interaction and task with awareness, treating each as an opportunity to reflect their life purpose. Whether through kind words, focused work, or acts of service, the seeker's purpose flows through their actions, creating a sense of coherence and unity within their life.

To deepen this integration, Metatron introduces the practice of reflecting on the motivations behind desires and goals. The seeker is encouraged to explore their aspirations, asking questions such as, "Is this in alignment with my highest self?" or "How does this serve my growth and others?" This introspective process helps the seeker differentiate between desires rooted in external expectations and those that arise from their authentic calling. Metatron's guidance brings clarity to this reflection, helping the seeker shape goals that are congruent with their spiritual path, resulting in a life that reflects their unique purpose in every pursuit.

In connecting further with purpose, Metatron introduces the seeker to the concept of aligning with a "higher vision"—a sense of purpose that extends beyond personal fulfillment and embraces service to others and the greater whole. Metatron teaches that purpose reaches its full power when it connects the individual with collective well-being, a calling that transcends personal boundaries and resonates with universal truth. The seeker is encouraged to visualize their life as a source of light that touches others, feeling the ripple effect of their purpose extending outward to inspire, heal, and uplift. This vision transforms life purpose into a shared journey, connecting the seeker with a deeper sense of unity and love.

To support this higher vision, Metatron offers a practice of creating a "purpose affirmation," a personalized statement that encapsulates the seeker's deepest values and aspirations. This affirmation, when spoken with conviction, becomes a beacon, helping the seeker remain focused on their spiritual path. Metatron encourages the seeker to repeat this affirmation daily, grounding their intentions in words that hold the essence of their calling. For example, a purpose affirmation might be, "I am here to bring light, to grow in wisdom, and to serve others with compassion." Through this repetition, the affirmation anchors the seeker in a state of purpose, attuning their mind and heart to the vibration of their true path.

In this phase of discovery, Metatron also emphasizes the importance of resilience, reminding the seeker that the path of purpose is not always straightforward. Challenges, doubts, and setbacks are natural parts of the journey and serve as opportunities to strengthen the connection to purpose. Metatron teaches the seeker to view these obstacles as moments of growth, where their commitment to purpose is refined and tested. With Metatron's light as a guide, the seeker learns to navigate these moments with patience and trust, knowing that each challenge contributes to their unfolding path. This resilience transforms purpose into a steadfast inner compass, one that remains steady regardless of external circumstances.

Metatron also introduces the seeker to the practice of connecting with nature as a means to renew and strengthen purpose. Nature, with its cycles of growth, decay, and rebirth, reflects the journey of purpose—a continuous evolution that adapts and transforms. The seeker is encouraged to spend time outdoors, observing the rhythm of natural life as a mirror for their own path. By aligning with the earth's cycles, they feel a sense of grounding and renewal, a reminder that purpose, like nature, has its seasons of change and renewal. Metatron's presence infuses these moments in nature, helping the seeker absorb the strength, peace, and clarity found in the natural world.

To cultivate an even deeper connection to purpose, Metatron introduces the practice of "purpose journaling," a reflective exercise that encourages the seeker to document their experiences, insights, and questions about their path. Each entry becomes an opportunity to explore how purpose is unfolding, to examine any shifts in desires or motivations, and to celebrate moments of alignment. Metatron's guidance in this practice transforms the journal into a sacred space, a record of the seeker's evolving purpose, offering clarity and insight. Over time, these reflections reveal patterns, themes, and revelations, deepening the seeker's understanding of their calling and fostering a continuous dialogue with the soul.

Metatron guides the seeker in recognizing and honoring the purpose of others, a practice that cultivates respect, empathy, and unity. By observing and honoring the diverse purposes of those around them, the seeker strengthens their own path, recognizing that each soul's journey contributes to the larger tapestry of existence. This awareness encourages the seeker to offer support, kindness, and understanding, fostering relationships that are grounded in mutual growth and spiritual respect. Metatron's guidance in this practice reveals that the journey of purpose is not a solitary one but is interwoven with the lives and paths of others, creating a shared experience of growth and enlightenment.

Through each of these practices, Metatron shows that life purpose is a living force, an essence that grows and transforms alongside the seeker. Purpose, when embraced fully, shapes not only what one does but how one experiences the world, grounding each action, thought, and relationship in alignment with the divine. The seeker, guided by Metatron, comes to understand that life purpose is a continual unfolding, a journey of discovering, embodying, and expressing the soul's unique light in a way that serves both self and the greater whole.

In this state of alignment, the seeker experiences a profound sense of peace and fulfillment, a knowing that each step, no matter how small, contributes to a greater purpose. With Metatron's presence, life purpose becomes not a goal to achieve but a truth to embody, a path of love, service, and wisdom that transforms every moment into an expression of the soul's highest calling. Through this journey, the seeker is empowered to live with authenticity, courage, and joy, fulfilling their role in the intricate, divine tapestry of life.

Chapter 11
Spiritual Self-Healing

The journey of spiritual self-healing reveals to the seeker that within lies a wellspring of renewal and resilience, capable of restoring both the body and the soul. With Archangel Metatron's guidance, the seeker learns that self-healing is not only about mending wounds but also about cultivating a harmonious state of being, where inner peace and strength coexist. Healing, as Metatron imparts, begins by looking within, embracing each aspect of oneself with compassion and recognizing that true healing is an alignment with the soul's highest energy.

Metatron begins by guiding the seeker to cultivate self-awareness, a foundational step in the self-healing process. Self-awareness, in this context, is the practice of observing one's thoughts, emotions, and physical sensations without judgment. Through this observation, the seeker becomes attuned to areas of tension, patterns of thought, and emotional blockages that might indicate imbalance or unhealed wounds. Metatron encourages the seeker to explore these inner landscapes with kindness, understanding that healing begins not with force but with gentle acceptance of what arises.

In this exploration, Metatron introduces the seeker to the art of connecting with the breath. Breath, as a bridge between body and spirit, is a powerful tool for calming the mind and opening channels of healing energy. Metatron guides the seeker in a breathing exercise, where each inhale draws in light and peace, while each exhale releases tension and emotional residue. This rhythmic breathing cultivates a sense of inner calm, preparing the body and mind to receive healing. The seeker learns to focus on each breath as a cycle of renewal, a simple yet profound practice that brings peace to areas where anxiety or stress might have taken hold.

With this grounding, Metatron invites the seeker to turn inward, visualizing a bright, healing light within the heart center. This light, infused with Metatron's energy, begins to expand, illuminating every part of the body and mind. As it spreads, this light dissolves any blockages, releasing feelings of heaviness or pain that may have lingered within. Metatron's presence is felt as a calming energy, a source of strength that assists the seeker in allowing this light to reach even the deepest parts of their being. In this state, the seeker experiences a profound connection to their inner healing power, recognizing that this light within is always available as a source of renewal.

To deepen the healing journey, Metatron introduces the seeker to the practice of "energy scanning," an exercise for identifying areas of the body or spirit that may need focused attention. The seeker is guided to pass their awareness through each part of their body, sensing any areas that feel heavy, tense, or resistant. By acknowledging these sensations without resistance, the seeker allows the healing process to unfold naturally. Metatron's guidance illuminates these areas, helping the seeker to feel supported and understood, knowing that healing is not a destination but an ongoing journey of tending to the soul.

In addition to physical self-awareness, Metatron emphasizes the healing of emotions, encouraging the seeker to explore unprocessed feelings that may be held within. These emotions, whether sadness, anger, or fear, are gently invited into awareness, where they can be acknowledged and released. Metatron encourages the seeker to view each emotion as a messenger, a reflection of experiences that have shaped them. Through compassionate self-acceptance, these emotions are allowed to surface and dissipate, clearing space for peace and vitality. This release creates a sense of lightness, as though layers of accumulated weight are lifted, allowing the seeker's true essence to shine more brightly.

Metatron further guides the seeker in practicing self-forgiveness, a powerful tool in spiritual self-healing. Self-forgiveness releases the burdens of regret, guilt, or self-judgment, replacing them with compassion and understanding. Metatron's energy envelops the seeker in a gentle, reassuring embrace, helping them to see past mistakes or perceived failures as steps along the journey, each offering valuable lessons. The seeker is encouraged to forgive not only past actions but also judgments or limitations placed upon themselves. This forgiveness opens the heart, creating a space where love and acceptance can heal the wounds of the past, allowing the seeker to move forward with renewed strength.

To support this journey of healing, Metatron introduces the practice of healing affirmations, positive statements that reinforce the seeker's intention to cultivate wholeness and well-being. The seeker is guided to choose affirmations such as "I am worthy of healing," "I embrace peace and release all that no longer serves me," or "My body, mind, and spirit are in harmony." Spoken with sincerity, these affirmations reprogram the mind, creating an inner atmosphere where healing can flourish. Metatron's energy amplifies these affirmations, allowing their power to resonate deeply within, reinforcing the seeker's commitment to their own well-being.

Metatron also emphasizes the importance of grounding this healing energy within the physical body. To support this, the seeker is encouraged to adopt grounding practices, such as walking barefoot on the earth, connecting with nature, or practicing mindful movement. These activities reinforce the connection between the body and the earth, creating a stable foundation for healing. Metatron's presence in these moments of grounding allows the seeker to feel secure and balanced, anchoring the healing energy into the physical form and supporting the natural flow of life force.

Metatron teaches the seeker the importance of patience and kindness on the journey of self-healing. Healing, he reveals, is not an instant transformation but a gradual process that requires dedication and gentleness. There may be days when progress feels slow, or emotions seem overwhelming, yet Metatron reassures the seeker that each step forward is a testament to their resilience and strength. He encourages the seeker to honor every part of their journey, knowing that each moment of healing, however small, contributes to a deeper state of inner peace and spiritual alignment.

Through these practices, the seeker comes to understand that self-healing is not about erasing pain but about embracing the full spectrum of one's experiences with love and awareness. Metatron's guidance illuminates the path of healing as a sacred return to wholeness, where each breath, each moment of forgiveness, and each act of self-compassion brings the seeker closer to their true essence. In this journey, healing becomes a state of grace, an ever-present reminder that within lies the power to restore, renew, and transform.

With Metatron's light as a constant companion, the seeker learns to live as their own healer, empowered to create a life of balance, harmony, and spiritual clarity. Through this path of self-healing, the seeker not only heals past wounds but discovers a profound source of inner peace, one that radiates outward, touching every aspect of their existence with love and purpose.

As the seeker delves further into the journey of self-healing, Archangel Metatron offers advanced practices that awaken and refine the body's natural energy centers, guiding the seeker to release deeper layers of emotional and energetic blockages. Healing, Metatron reveals, is a dynamic process—a continuous realignment of the physical, emotional, and spiritual bodies to the frequencies of peace and balance. The seeker's focus shifts from healing as a destination to an active, daily engagement with the soul's energy, a process that transforms inner wounds into powerful sources of resilience and insight.

Metatron begins by teaching the seeker the practice of "energy transmutation," a technique that uses visualization to shift stagnant or negative energy into light. The seeker is guided to visualize any heavy or uncomfortable energy within as a dark cloud, noticing where it resides and observing it with compassion. Through Metatron's guidance, this cloud is gradually transformed, illuminated by a golden or violet light, which dissolves the heaviness and clears the energy. This transmutation process is enhanced by Metatron's presence, as his light permeates the seeker's being, assisting in lifting the remaining weight and converting it into a state of clarity and calm.

To deepen the clearing of emotional and energetic blockages, Metatron introduces the practice of chakra-focused healing, where the seeker uses awareness to release and balance energy within specific chakras. The seeker is encouraged to focus on one chakra at a time, beginning with the root, and working upward through each energy center. For each chakra, Metatron guides the seeker in visualizing a radiant light specific to that chakra's color, breathing into it and sensing any areas of tension or imbalance. As they continue to breathe, Metatron's energy merges with theirs, helping to dissolve any blockages and bringing the chakra back to its natural state of vibrant flow. This practice not only clears blockages but reinforces a harmonious alignment among all the chakras, grounding the healing energy throughout the entire being.

In addition to chakra-focused healing, Metatron introduces the seeker to guided meditation as a method of self-awareness and emotional release. The seeker is guided to settle into a state of deep relaxation, focusing inward, and connecting with emotions that may have been suppressed or ignored. Metatron's presence creates a safe and compassionate environment, where the seeker can gently bring these emotions to the surface. Whether sadness, fear, anger, or grief, each feeling is invited into awareness without judgment, allowing it to be acknowledged, expressed, and finally released. This emotional release brings a sense of profound relief, as the seeker no longer carries the weight of unexpressed emotions, making space for peace and acceptance to fill the heart.

To support ongoing healing, Metatron introduces the seeker to the practice of mantra repetition, using specific sounds or phrases to promote internal harmony. Mantras, as Metatron teaches, are powerful vibrational tools that connect the seeker with divine energies, clearing and purifying the mind and spirit. The seeker is encouraged to select a mantra that resonates with their intentions for healing, such as "I am whole," "I am at peace," or "I release and renew." Through consistent repetition, this mantra becomes a subtle yet powerful healing force, gently recalibrating the seeker's energy to align with their highest self. With Metatron's guidance, the mantra becomes an anchor, allowing the seeker to access the healing energy at any moment, regardless of external circumstances.

Metatron further guides the seeker in grounding these healing practices through a ritual of gratitude, reminding them of the profound connection between gratitude and self-healing. Each evening, the seeker is encouraged to take a few moments to reflect on the healing journey, acknowledging every small step, insight, or release that has taken place. Metatron's light fills this moment of reflection, amplifying the seeker's gratitude and reinforcing their connection with the healing process. This gratitude ritual becomes an affirmation of self-love, a recognition of the courage and dedication that self-healing requires, and a reminder that healing is a continuous, compassionate journey.

To integrate these practices into daily life, Metatron introduces "soul alignment," a practice of aligning actions and choices with the energy of wholeness and wellness. Through this practice, the seeker is encouraged to tune into their inner wisdom when making decisions, asking, "Does this align with my highest good? Will this bring balance and healing to my being?" This mindfulness extends to lifestyle choices, relationships, and personal habits, creating a life that supports, rather than detracts from, the healing journey. Metatron's guidance in this alignment practice allows the seeker to live in a state of harmony, where each action reinforces the ongoing process of self-healing.

Metatron introduces the seeker to a visualization known as "the mirror of compassion." In this visualization, the seeker imagines looking into a mirror that reflects not only their current self but also the essence of who they are becoming—a whole, peaceful, and balanced being. Metatron's light surrounds this mirror, revealing the seeker's true self, healed and complete. In this state, the seeker observes with compassion, free from judgment or self-criticism, recognizing that each part of their journey has contributed to their growth. This reflection becomes a powerful reminder of the inner strength that healing has awakened, reinforcing a commitment to nurturing their well-being in every moment.

Through each of these advanced practices, the seeker discovers that self-healing is a holistic journey—one that encompasses mind, body, and spirit. With Metatron's guidance, self-healing becomes a dynamic, living process, an engagement with one's true self that transforms pain into understanding, and wounds into wisdom. The seeker learns that within lies an infinite capacity to heal, a reservoir of light and resilience that shines brighter with each act of self-compassion, forgiveness, and gratitude.

Metatron's presence serves as a gentle but powerful reminder that healing is an expression of love for oneself, a path that brings the seeker into alignment with the soul's natural state of peace. As this journey continues, the seeker comes to understand that true self-healing is not an end, but a journey of becoming—a process of remembering one's inherent wholeness, of embracing each part of oneself with kindness, and of walking forward with renewed strength, clarity, and purpose. Through this path of self-healing, the seeker not only transforms their inner world but radiates a light that uplifts, inspires, and heals others along the way.

Chapter 12
Connection with Nature

In the unfolding journey of spiritual awareness, Archangel Metatron guides the seeker into a deeper communion with nature, revealing the earth itself as a boundless source of energy, balance, and healing. This connection with nature is not simply a physical experience; it is an alignment with the rhythms and cycles of life that mirror the spiritual journey. Nature, in its quiet majesty, offers the seeker a path to grounding, renewal, and a sense of unity with all creation. Through this connection, the seeker finds not only solace but an awakening to the sacredness of life itself.

Metatron begins by inviting the seeker to enter nature with reverence, seeing each tree, stone, river, and mountain as a living entity resonating with energy. The earth is not merely a landscape to be observed but a realm to be experienced, a presence that nurtures, teaches, and restores. In moments of quiet observation, the seeker is encouraged to feel this aliveness, allowing themselves to slow down, breathe deeply, and attune to the pulse of the natural world. Through Metatron's guidance, this act of attunement becomes a ritual of respect, a way of honoring the earth as both home and teacher.

To deepen this connection, Metatron introduces the practice of "grounding," a technique that aligns the seeker's energy with the stabilizing force of the earth. Grounding involves standing barefoot on natural earth—soil, sand, or grass—and feeling a connection with the ground below. The seeker is guided to visualize roots extending from the soles of their feet, reaching deep into the earth's core, where they absorb the earth's energy.

As these roots anchor and strengthen, the seeker feels a sense of stability, as though the earth itself is supporting them, holding them steady. Metatron's presence reinforces this grounding, allowing the seeker to release anxieties and tensions into the earth, which absorbs and transforms them, creating a foundation of balance and calm.

In this state of grounding, Metatron encourages the seeker to engage in the practice of "breathing with nature." This exercise, simple yet profound, involves harmonizing one's breath with the rhythms of the natural world. Seated quietly among trees or near a body of water, the seeker focuses on each breath, imagining they are inhaling the life force of the earth and exhaling any inner heaviness. As this rhythmic breathing continues, a natural exchange unfolds—each inhale draws in the revitalizing energy of nature, while each exhale releases anything that no longer serves the seeker's highest good. This connection through breath opens the seeker to the nurturing qualities of nature, a reminder of the harmony that exists between all living things.

Metatron then introduces the practice of "elemental connection," where the seeker experiences the unique energies of the natural elements—earth, water, fire, and air. Each element holds qualities that resonate with different aspects of the seeker's spirit, inviting them into a state of balance and wholeness. The seeker is encouraged to touch the earth to feel grounded, to listen to flowing water to cultivate emotional release, to bask in sunlight for vitality, and to feel the breeze as a cleansing force that clears the mind. Metatron's guidance allows the seeker to experience each element as a reflection of their own nature, helping them to understand that they, too, carry the resilience of the earth, the fluidity of water, the warmth of fire, and the freedom of air.

Through Metatron's guidance, the seeker also explores the concept of "tree communion," an ancient practice of connecting with trees to receive their wisdom and energy. In this exercise, the seeker is encouraged to approach a tree with respect, resting their hand against its trunk, feeling its bark, and closing their eyes to sense its presence. The seeker is guided to breathe with the tree, allowing their energies to synchronize, feeling the slow, steady heartbeat of the tree, which mirrors the calm patience of the earth. Metatron's light surrounds this communion, amplifying the sense of connection and offering the seeker insights or impressions that arise from this quiet exchange. In the presence of the tree, the seeker feels grounded, calm, and renewed, sensing the silent wisdom of a life that has witnessed seasons and cycles beyond human measure.

Metatron further introduces the practice of "nature journaling," a reflective exercise in which the seeker captures the insights, emotions, and experiences that arise during time spent in nature. Each entry becomes a space for the seeker to express gratitude, to document moments of peace or inspiration, and to note any changes in perspective. Through this journaling, the seeker creates a record of their connection with the earth, a reminder of the growth and healing that nature facilitates. Metatron's presence in this process allows each entry to become a form of spiritual dialogue, where the insights received from nature deepen the seeker's understanding of their own journey.

In moments of stillness, Metatron guides the seeker to observe the cycles of nature as symbols of their own spiritual path. The changing seasons, the rise and fall of tides, and the daily arc of the sun each reflect the natural rhythm of growth, transformation, and renewal. Metatron encourages the seeker to attune to these cycles, finding within them a source of peace and patience. Just as nature moves through seasons of abundance and rest, the seeker learns to accept their own periods of growth and stillness, trusting that each phase contributes to the wholeness of their journey. This reflection cultivates a sense of ease and acceptance, a knowing that they are part of a vast, interconnected flow.

To conclude this part of the journey, Metatron introduces the seeker to the practice of offering gratitude to the earth. Before leaving any natural setting, the seeker is encouraged to pause, bowing their head or placing a hand on the ground as an act of acknowledgment. This simple gesture of gratitude honors the earth as a source of life and a partner in the journey of spiritual awakening. Metatron's presence fills this moment, creating a sacred space of mutual respect between the seeker and the earth, a reminder that all of creation is connected in a shared dance of life.

Through each of these practices, the seeker comes to understand that connecting with nature is not only a source of healing but a return to a state of harmony with the world. With Metatron's guidance, nature becomes more than a backdrop to life; it transforms into a living temple, a reflection of the divine that supports, heals, and teaches. This connection with the earth grounds the seeker's spirit, offering them the wisdom to live in balance, resilience, and peace.

In this communion with nature, the seeker discovers a sense of belonging—a profound realization that they are part of a greater whole, a life that extends beyond individuality to encompass all of creation. Through this connection, the seeker moves forward with a heart that is open, a mind that is still, and a spirit that walks in harmony with the natural world, supported by the ever-present light of Metatron.

As the seeker deepens their connection with nature, Archangel Metatron reveals advanced practices that enable them to engage more profoundly with the elements and energies of the natural world. Nature, as Metatron teaches, is a bridge to spiritual alignment, a space where the soul finds not only peace but a powerful source of vitality. Through these practices, the seeker learns to attune to the earth's energy with greater sensitivity, using it as a wellspring of balance, strength, and renewal.

Metatron introduces the practice of "grounding visualization," a technique that allows the seeker to draw strength directly from the earth's core. Seated on natural ground, the seeker visualizes roots extending from their spine or feet deep into the earth, connecting with its core's vibrant energy. This energy, warm and nourishing, begins to rise through the roots, filling the seeker's body with a steady, grounding force. With each breath, this energy flows upward, bringing a sense of stability and calm to the mind and spirit. Metatron's guidance amplifies this grounding energy, helping the seeker to release any accumulated tension or stress, grounding them in the present moment with a renewed sense of clarity and peace.

To enhance the alignment with nature's energy, Metatron introduces "elemental attunement," a practice that goes beyond merely observing the elements to embodying their qualities. For earth, the seeker is encouraged to touch the soil, feeling its stability and strength. With water, they may hold their hands under a flowing stream or visualize themselves immersed in calm, cleansing waters, releasing emotions that need healing. Fire is experienced as warmth from sunlight or the glow of a candle, instilling vitality and courage. Air, represented by a breeze or open sky, is drawn into the lungs with each breath, bringing freedom and fresh perspective. Through Metatron's guidance, this attunement becomes a way of harmonizing with nature's cycles, allowing the elements to work as healers and allies on the path of spiritual growth.

In this state of connection, Metatron introduces the seeker to the concept of "receiving messages from nature," a practice of intuitive listening where the seeker opens themselves to the subtle language of the natural world. The seeker is encouraged to approach nature with curiosity and openness, observing animals, plants, or even the patterns of clouds and sensing if a particular sight or sound resonates with them. Metatron teaches that nature communicates in symbols and impressions, and by tuning into this quiet language, the seeker may receive insights, guidance, or reminders from the earth's wisdom. Whether it's the appearance of a specific animal, the gentle rustle of leaves, or the call of a distant bird, each moment carries a message, a whisper of guidance that aligns with the seeker's inner journey.

To deepen this intuitive connection, Metatron introduces the seeker to "tree meditation," a practice of merging energy with a tree's essence to access its wisdom and strength. The seeker selects a tree that resonates with them, placing both hands on its trunk and closing their eyes. As they focus on their breath, they visualize their energy merging with the tree's slow, grounded rhythm, feeling the solidity and patience it embodies. Metatron's presence enhances this connection, allowing the seeker to experience the tree's energy as a grounding force that calms and centers. This meditation fosters resilience and provides a reminder of the timeless patience that characterizes the natural world, a lesson in the power of stillness and rootedness.

Metatron also guides the seeker through the practice of "sun and moon bathing," a ritual of absorbing energy directly from celestial bodies. During sunlight hours, the seeker is encouraged to stand under the sun, eyes closed, allowing the warmth and light to fill them with vitality and strength. In contrast, moon bathing involves standing under the moonlight, letting its cool, reflective light wash over them, bringing a sense of calm and introspection. Sun and moonlight each carry unique energies—the sun invigorates and energizes, while the moon soothes and heals. Metatron's guidance allows the seeker to experience these energies as complementary forces that bring balance, a harmony between action and reflection, warmth and coolness, strength and gentleness.

In times when the seeker feels disconnected or overwhelmed, Metatron introduces the practice of "earthing," a grounding ritual that uses the earth's magnetic field to reset the seeker's energy. Walking barefoot on natural ground, whether grass, sand, or soil, the seeker visualizes themselves absorbing the earth's natural frequency, feeling it harmonize with their own. This practice creates a powerful grounding effect, dispelling residual stress and promoting mental clarity. Metatron's energy is present throughout, helping the seeker feel supported and embraced by the earth's nurturing energy. Earthing becomes a reminder of the body's natural connection to the planet, a source of calm and stability accessible at any time.

Metatron also introduces "nature-inspired journaling," a practice that involves recording impressions, insights, or visions that emerge while in nature. The seeker may bring a journal into the natural world, pausing periodically to note thoughts, emotions, or sensations. Metatron's guidance helps the seeker recognize patterns in these reflections, seeing how nature's messages align with their personal growth. Each entry becomes a space for the seeker to honor the guidance received, creating a dialogue between themselves and the natural world. Over time, this journal becomes a personal record of growth, capturing how nature's wisdom has woven into the seeker's path, a testament to the healing presence of the earth.

As the seeker grows more attuned to nature, Metatron teaches them to give back to the earth in small, meaningful ways, transforming gratitude into action. Whether it's planting a tree, cleaning a natural area, or simply offering a prayer of thanks, these acts of reciprocity strengthen the bond with nature, creating a cycle of giving and receiving. Metatron's presence in these moments reinforces the understanding that spiritual connection with nature is a shared relationship, a commitment to nurture the earth as it nurtures the soul. This reciprocity deepens the seeker's alignment with the natural world, transforming their connection into a partnership grounded in mutual respect and care.

Through these practices, the seeker experiences nature as a wellspring of spiritual support, a source of both inner peace and strength. With Metatron's guidance, nature becomes a sanctuary, a living presence that grounds, renews, and inspires the spirit. Each interaction with the earth, each moment spent in communion with its elements, becomes a step toward balance and wholeness, a deepening of the spiritual journey that unites the seeker with the cycles of life itself.

This connection with nature transforms the seeker's perspective, helping them to walk with a heart open to the beauty and wisdom that surrounds them, grounded in the earth and inspired by the heavens. In this alignment, the seeker moves forward with a sense of unity, a recognition that they are both part of and supported by the natural world, embraced by the earth as they continue their journey toward spiritual fulfillment.

Chapter 13
Intuition and Wisdom

As the journey deepens, Archangel Metatron introduces the seeker to intuition as a vital aspect of spiritual development, a guiding light within that transcends logic and intellect. Intuition, as Metatron teaches, is the voice of the soul, an ancient wisdom that lies beneath words, carrying the seeker into realms of understanding that align with their true essence. This inner voice, when awakened and trusted, becomes a powerful tool for growth, a source of insight that connects the seeker not only to their path but to the universal truths woven into the fabric of existence.

Metatron begins by guiding the seeker to recognize the quiet nature of intuition. Unlike thoughts, which may race and collide, intuition is a subtle, often gentle knowing—a sensation, image, or insight that arises without force. The seeker is encouraged to create moments of silence, allowing intuition the space to emerge without interference. In these quiet moments, Metatron's energy surrounds the seeker, amplifying the sense of calm and clarity needed for intuition to surface. Each intuitive nudge, however small, is treated as a gift, a message from the soul that leads the seeker closer to a life of authenticity and purpose.

One of the first practices Metatron introduces is "intuitive listening," a mindful approach to everyday experiences that trains the seeker to recognize and trust their intuition. The seeker is guided to notice their immediate reactions to choices, people, or environments, asking themselves, "What is my first feeling? What subtle impressions arise?" This practice of paying attention to initial responses—before thoughts or judgments intrude—enables the seeker to hear their intuition as it speaks. Metatron's guidance in this practice strengthens the seeker's confidence, helping them to distinguish between intuition and thought, to sense which impressions are the soul's whispers and which arise from the mind's conditioning.

To further develop intuitive abilities, Metatron introduces "visualization practices," exercises that allow the seeker to expand their inner vision and receive guidance through images or symbols. In these visualizations, the seeker is encouraged to pose a question or reflect on an area of their life where they seek clarity, allowing any images or symbols that arise to appear naturally. Metatron's energy infuses the visualization, guiding the seeker to interpret these symbols with openness and curiosity. Each symbol, whether a landscape, color, or form, is seen as a language unique to the seeker's inner world. Through these visualizations, the seeker learns to decode the symbols of intuition, understanding that this language is as individual as their journey.

Metatron then guides the seeker to use meditation as a powerful practice for tuning into intuition, quieting the mind to reveal the soul's voice. In meditation, the seeker focuses on their breath, allowing thoughts to settle until a sense of inner stillness emerges. In this state, Metatron's presence serves as a beacon, a source of light that invites intuitive insights to come forward. During these meditative sessions, the seeker may experience moments of clarity, as though answers and understanding are gently unveiled. Metatron encourages the seeker to welcome these impressions, even if they are vague or partial, trusting that each piece will reveal its full meaning over time.

To encourage the development of intuitive wisdom, Metatron introduces "the practice of feeling resonance," an exercise that involves sensing the alignment or dissonance of choices or situations with the seeker's core truth. In moments of decision-making, the seeker is guided to place their hand over their heart and ask, "Does this feel right? Is there a lightness or heaviness here?" This practice goes beyond intellectual reasoning, bringing the seeker into alignment with their energetic responses. Through Metatron's support, the seeker becomes attuned to the sensation of resonance, learning to move toward choices that feel harmonious and true while gently releasing those that feel misaligned.

To deepen the journey, Metatron introduces the seeker to the concept of "listening to the body's wisdom." Physical sensations, he explains, are often intuitive signals—the tightening of muscles, a flutter in the chest, or a sense of calm can reveal insights that bypass words. The seeker learns to observe these responses, recognizing that their body, too, holds intuition and knowledge. With Metatron's encouragement, the seeker begins to trust these bodily cues, seeing them as messages from the inner self. Over time, this practice strengthens the connection between body, mind, and soul, creating an integrated system of wisdom that guides the seeker with clarity and balance.

In times of uncertainty, Metatron introduces "intuitive journaling" as a way to explore and process intuitive insights. In this practice, the seeker sits with a pen and journal, allowing their thoughts to flow freely onto the page. By writing without judgment or structure, the seeker creates space for hidden insights to emerge, often discovering clarity as they express their thoughts. Metatron's guidance brings a sense of peace to this practice, helping the seeker to trust the insights that arise. Over time, the journal becomes a record of intuitive moments and revelations, a personal testament to the unfolding wisdom within.

Metatron also guides the seeker in connecting intuition with wisdom gained from life experiences. He teaches that intuition is not an isolated gift but one that grows richer through the accumulation of knowledge, compassion, and understanding. The seeker is encouraged to reflect on past experiences, recognizing moments when intuition provided guidance that may have been overlooked. Through this reflection, the seeker learns to integrate intuition with life's lessons, creating a foundation of wisdom that strengthens their inner compass. Metatron's energy brings a sense of compassion to this process, reminding the seeker that every experience, whether joyful or challenging, adds depth to their intuitive abilities.

Through each of these practices, the seeker awakens to the profound wisdom that lies within, a source of guidance that flows from the soul. With Metatron's presence, intuition becomes a trusted ally, a voice that offers insights, protection, and clarity along the spiritual path. The seeker learns that intuition is more than a fleeting sensation; it is a form of spiritual sight, a light that reveals the true nature of choices, relationships, and life's unfolding journey.

As this connection with intuition grows, the seeker experiences a greater sense of trust in themselves, an unwavering knowing that they are guided by something pure and timeless. This deepened relationship with intuition aligns the seeker more fully with their spiritual path, bringing a sense of harmony and inner peace as they navigate life's twists and turns. Through the cultivation of intuition and wisdom, Metatron reveals a journey of trust, clarity, and profound connection with the essence of the soul itself.

As the seeker delves further into the realms of intuition and wisdom, Archangel Metatron guides them in refining their intuitive abilities and cultivating practices that deepen their relationship with inner knowing. Intuition, as Metatron reveals, is a pathway to profound spiritual insight, an innate compass that grows stronger with trust and dedication. By embracing this guidance, the seeker learns to navigate their journey with greater clarity and openness, fostering a spiritual connection that transcends the boundaries of logic and awakens the wisdom within.

Metatron introduces the practice of "intuitive meditation," a technique that combines focused intention with deep listening. In a quiet space, the seeker is invited to enter a meditative state, focusing on a specific question or area of life where they seek guidance. Metatron's energy envelops the seeker, creating a supportive space where answers can arise naturally. Rather than seeking immediate clarity, the seeker learns to remain open, observing any images, emotions, or sensations that surface. Through this practice, the seeker becomes attuned to the subtle language of intuition, understanding that insights often appear as gentle whispers or sensations rather than direct answers.

To further develop their intuitive perception, Metatron introduces the seeker to "crystal work," incorporating stones known to amplify intuitive clarity, such as amethyst, labradorite, and clear quartz. Each crystal, as Metatron explains, carries a unique frequency that resonates with the seeker's inner guidance. The seeker is encouraged to hold a chosen crystal during meditation or place it near their heart, allowing its energy to enhance their intuitive connection. Metatron's presence heightens this experience, creating a harmonious exchange of energy that aligns the seeker with the crystal's purpose. Through repeated practice, the seeker begins to notice an increased sensitivity to intuitive insights, experiencing a sense of clarity that grows stronger over time.

Metatron then introduces the "mirror of inner truth," a visualization exercise designed to cultivate self-honesty, helping the seeker to see beyond illusions or self-imposed limitations. In this practice, the seeker envisions a mirror before them, reflecting their deepest truths and desires. As they gaze into this mirror, Metatron's light reveals aspects of their intuition that may have been obscured by fear, doubt, or external expectations. Through this honest reflection, the seeker is invited to recognize and release any hesitations that hold them back, allowing their intuitive wisdom to flow freely. This exercise not only strengthens intuition but also aligns the seeker with their authentic self, creating a path of clarity and self-acceptance.

Metatron also guides the seeker in developing a ritual with "mantras for intuition," specific phrases or words that help the mind tune into inner guidance. Mantras such as "I trust my inner voice," "My intuition guides me with clarity," or "I am open to the wisdom within" create a mental atmosphere of receptivity and trust. The seeker is encouraged to repeat their chosen mantra each day, infusing it with intention and focus. Over time, the repetition of these words strengthens the seeker's intuitive trust, allowing them to approach each situation with a deepened sense of inner knowing. Metatron's energy supports this practice, reinforcing the seeker's belief in their own guidance and fostering an unwavering sense of self-confidence.

To help the seeker listen more intently to intuition, Metatron introduces "listening stones," a practice of connecting with stones as conduits for intuitive messages. The seeker is invited to select a stone that resonates with them, holding it gently in their hands as they ask a question or seek insight. As they listen, the seeker is encouraged to notice any subtle sensations, thoughts, or impressions that arise. Through this practice, the seeker learns to tap into the ancient wisdom carried by stones, experiencing nature as a source of guidance and healing. Metatron's presence strengthens the seeker's connection to these energies, allowing them to access insights that feel grounded and clear, free from external influence.

Metatron further introduces "body-centered intuition," a practice of tuning into physical sensations as expressions of intuitive wisdom. In moments of decision or contemplation, the seeker is guided to observe any changes in their body—tightness, warmth, ease, or resistance—as signals from their inner self. Metatron teaches that the body often senses the truth before the mind can process it, acting as an intuitive guide in its own right. Through this practice, the seeker learns to trust these physical responses, treating them as valuable information on their spiritual journey. Over time, this alignment with the body's wisdom strengthens the seeker's ability to make decisions that resonate with their soul's purpose.

To deepen the seeker's intuitive vision, Metatron introduces "scrying with water," an ancient practice that involves gazing into a bowl of water to receive symbolic messages. The seeker is encouraged to fill a clear bowl with water, setting it in a quiet, dimly lit space. With focused intention, they gaze into the water's surface, allowing any images or impressions to come forth. Metatron's energy surrounds this practice, creating a space where the seeker feels safe and open to receive. This water scrying invites intuitive images and impressions to emerge, encouraging the seeker to trust in the spontaneous messages that appear. Each session offers a glimpse into the seeker's inner vision, enhancing their ability to perceive beyond the ordinary.

As intuition deepens, Metatron guides the seeker in "attuning to universal signs," a practice of observing synchronicities and subtle messages in daily life. Metatron teaches that intuition often communicates through signs in the world—patterns, numbers, recurring themes, or encounters that carry specific meaning. The seeker is encouraged to notice these signs without overanalyzing, trusting that they hold insights aligned with their journey. Through Metatron's guidance, each sign becomes a bridge between the seeker's inner wisdom and the universe, reinforcing the connection between their intuitive knowing and the energies surrounding them. This attunement to signs fosters a sense of interconnectedness, allowing the seeker to feel supported by the universe at every step.

To close this exploration, Metatron introduces the seeker to "journaling with crystals," a practice that combines intuitive journaling with the energy of a chosen crystal. Holding the crystal as they write, the seeker is encouraged to express their thoughts and feelings freely, allowing the crystal's energy to amplify their intuitive flow. Metatron's presence in this practice brings a heightened sense of awareness, helping the seeker access deeper layers of insight and wisdom. Each journal entry becomes a sacred dialogue between the seeker and their inner self, a place where the truths revealed through intuition find expression and clarity. This practice deepens the seeker's relationship with their intuition, creating a personal record of growth and discovery that can be revisited over time.

Through each of these advanced practices, the seeker's intuition becomes a steady, reliable guide, a source of wisdom that harmonizes with their soul's path. With Metatron's guidance, the seeker learns that intuition is not separate from wisdom but a manifestation of it, a language that speaks to the heart and mind in ways that logic cannot fully capture. By embracing intuition, the seeker discovers a path of alignment with their truest self, an inner clarity that shines through every choice, experience, and connection.

Metatron's teachings remind the seeker that intuition is a gift to be nurtured, a bridge between the seen and unseen, a light that illuminates the way forward. With each step, the seeker moves with confidence, grounded in a wisdom that is timeless, a knowing that originates from the soul's deepest truth. Through this journey, the seeker grows in strength, trust, and peace, fully aligned with the quiet yet profound voice within.

Chapter 14
Chakra Cleansing

As the seeker journeys further into spiritual alignment, Archangel Metatron reveals the importance of a regular practice of chakra cleansing. Each chakra, a vital energy center within the body, plays a unique role in maintaining balance between physical, emotional, and spiritual aspects of life. When energy flows freely through the chakras, the seeker experiences harmony and alignment; when blockages form, they can disrupt this flow, leading to emotional or physical strain. Cleansing the chakras is a sacred act of renewal, a way to restore the energy body to its natural state of openness and clarity.

Metatron begins by guiding the seeker to understand the fundamental purpose of each chakra. The root chakra, located at the base of the spine, grounds the seeker, connecting them to stability, safety, and physical well-being. The sacral chakra, centered below the navel, governs creativity, passion, and emotional flow. The solar plexus chakra, just above the navel, is the seat of personal power, confidence, and self-worth. The heart chakra, in the center of the chest, embodies love, compassion, and connection. The throat chakra, at the throat's base, enables clear expression and communication. The third eye chakra, between the eyebrows, provides inner vision, intuition, and insight. The crown chakra, at the top of the head, opens the seeker to divine consciousness and universal energy.

With this awareness, Metatron introduces the seeker to a simple yet profound cleansing technique, the "chakra visualization." In a quiet space, the seeker is guided to sit comfortably, focusing on their breath to quiet the mind.

Beginning with the root chakra, Metatron instructs the seeker to visualize each chakra as a spinning wheel of light, radiating its respective color: red for the root, orange for the sacral, yellow for the solar plexus, green or pink for the heart, blue for the throat, indigo for the third eye, and violet or white for the crown. As each chakra is visualized, Metatron's light surrounds it, purifying and energizing, dissolving any heaviness or stagnation. This visualization brings a renewed sense of vitality, as if each chakra is infused with pure, healing energy.

To deepen the cleansing process, Metatron introduces the practice of "breathwork for chakra purification." With this technique, the seeker focuses on each chakra individually, breathing in deeply and directing the breath to that chakra, imagining it expanding with light. On each exhale, any dense or stagnant energy is released, dissipating into the air. Beginning at the root and moving up to the crown, this breathwork practice transforms each chakra, renewing its energy and clearing blockages. Metatron's presence enhances the effectiveness of this practice, creating a cocoon of protective light around the seeker as each breath draws them closer to a state of balance and inner calm.

In addition to visualization and breathwork, Metatron introduces the seeker to the use of sound as a tool for chakra cleansing. Each chakra resonates with a particular frequency, and by chanting or listening to the associated sound, the seeker can bring that chakra into alignment. The root chakra resonates with the sound "LAM," the sacral with "VAM," the solar plexus with "RAM," the heart with "YAM," the throat with "HAM," the third eye with "OM," and the crown with a silent vibration or the sound of "AUM." By chanting or listening to these sounds, the seeker feels each chakra vibrating in harmony with its natural frequency, allowing energy to flow freely. With Metatron's guidance, this practice becomes a ritual of attunement, where sound acts as a bridge between physical and spiritual realms, lifting and realigning the seeker's energy field.

Metatron then introduces the seeker to the cleansing power of nature, encouraging them to spend time in natural settings to reset their energy. Standing barefoot on grass, touching a tree, or sitting near running water, the seeker can absorb the earth's grounding energy, which naturally clears and stabilizes the chakras. Metatron's presence amplifies this connection, allowing the seeker to feel the cleansing effect of the earth, which draws away negative energies and restores equilibrium. Through this practice, the seeker learns to use nature as a resource, a living presence that nurtures and balances the energy centers, creating a state of harmony within.

To further enhance chakra cleansing, Metatron introduces the seeker to the use of water as a purification tool. The seeker is encouraged to visualize water flowing through each chakra, washing away any blockages or impurities. This can be done during a shower or bath, where the seeker envisions the water as a gentle stream of light that carries away heaviness, leaving the chakras clear and vibrant. Metatron's light intensifies this cleansing, helping the seeker feel renewed, refreshed, and free from energetic burdens. Through this practice, the seeker comes to see water as a purifying force, one that not only cleanses the body but restores balance to the energy field.

In moments when the seeker feels particularly overwhelmed or blocked, Metatron introduces the technique of "hands-on energy clearing." The seeker is guided to place their hands over each chakra, beginning with the root, and to focus on sending warm, healing energy through their hands into the chakra. With each chakra, the seeker sets an intention of release, asking for any stagnant or negative energy to be lifted. Metatron's presence is felt through the warmth and peace that spreads from the hands to each chakra, creating a direct and powerful flow of healing energy. This hands-on approach brings a tangible sense of comfort and support, reminding the seeker of their own capacity to heal and restore.

Metatron teaches the importance of regular chakra cleansing as a foundation for spiritual health. Just as one maintains physical wellness, maintaining energetic hygiene through chakra cleansing keeps the spirit vibrant and resilient. The seeker learns that even small, daily practices—such as moments of deep breathing, a few minutes of visualization, or standing barefoot on the earth—are meaningful acts of self-care. Metatron's guidance infuses these practices with sacred intention, transforming them from routine tasks into rituals that nurture and uplift the soul.

Through each of these practices, the seeker experiences the power of chakra cleansing as a pathway to inner clarity and peace. With Metatron's presence, the seeker not only cleanses their energy centers but also deepens their understanding of each chakra's role in their life, discovering that these energy centers are more than points within the body; they are portals to self-awareness, healing, and transformation. Chakra cleansing, as Metatron reveals, is a continual renewal, a return to one's essential light, where the soul shines freely, unburdened, and connected to the divine flow of energy that sustains all life.

Guided by Archangel Metatron, the seeker now explores advanced techniques for achieving a deep and lasting cleanse of each chakra. With Metatron's presence as a source of heightened awareness, the seeker learns that each energy center holds not only vibrational power but layers of emotional, mental, and spiritual energies that require attentive care. These advanced practices allow the seeker to reach deeper within, releasing not only recent blockages but also older, buried patterns that have shaped their energy flow over time.

Metatron introduces "crystal cleansing" as a potent tool for purifying and realigning each chakra. Crystals, with their unique frequencies, act as conduits for clearing stagnant energies while amplifying the natural qualities of each chakra. The seeker is guided to use specific stones, such as grounding black tourmaline for the root chakra, creativity-enhancing carnelian for the sacral, or confidence-boosting citrine for the solar plexus. Metatron teaches the seeker to place each crystal directly on the corresponding chakra while visualizing the stone's energy blending with their own, purifying, and restoring flow. The seeker feels the gentle power of the stones, sensing each chakra respond with openness and renewal as the crystal clears away density and recharges it with vibrant energy.

For a more profound cleanse, Metatron introduces "light infusion," a practice that involves envisioning beams of pure light pouring into each chakra to dissolve accumulated heaviness. The seeker visualizes a sphere of white or golden light above their head, representing Metatron's presence and divine healing energy. One by one, each chakra is bathed in this light, beginning with the root and ascending through to the crown. As this light touches each chakra, it clears and revitalizes the center, creating a channel that feels open, expansive, and deeply at peace. Through this process, the seeker senses Metatron's light penetrating beyond the surface, touching layers of each chakra where older emotional or energetic patterns may be stored. With each breath, the light dissolves these imprints, allowing the seeker to feel liberated and aligned with their inner truth.

Metatron next guides the seeker in using "essential oils for chakra balancing," an ancient technique that combines the subtle powers of scent and plant energy. The seeker is encouraged to anoint each chakra with a specific oil: grounding cedarwood for the root, sensual jasmine for the sacral, uplifting lemon for the solar plexus, rose for the heart, peppermint for the throat, lavender for the third eye, and frankincense for the crown. Each oil is chosen for its energetic resonance, enhancing the qualities of its associated chakra. Metatron's presence enhances the aromatic experience, creating a sensory bridge between the seeker's body, emotions, and spirit. As the fragrance lingers, it subtly shifts the vibrational field of each chakra, restoring a balanced flow that allows the seeker to feel connected, centered, and in tune with their energy body.

To further refine the energy, Metatron introduces "chakra chants," a vocal technique that aligns each chakra through sound resonance. By intoning specific sounds, the seeker tunes each energy center to its natural frequency, clearing away disruptions and strengthening the flow. Beginning at the root with the sound "LAM," the seeker moves upward through each chakra, chanting "VAM," "RAM," "YAM," "HAM," "OM," and finally a silent "AUM" for the crown. The vibrations from these sounds echo through the seeker's body, dissolving blockages and bringing the chakras into harmonious alignment. With Metatron's guidance, this practice becomes a deeply embodied experience, transforming sound into healing energy that resonates through every layer of the seeker's being.

Metatron also introduces "chakra journaling" as a reflective practice for uncovering deeper emotional or mental patterns that may be affecting each chakra's balance. The seeker is guided to reflect on each chakra individually, writing down feelings, memories, or beliefs that arise when focusing on that energy center. For instance, when journaling about the root chakra, the seeker might explore themes of safety, belonging, and stability. As they write, Metatron's presence provides clarity and support, encouraging the seeker to delve into these themes without judgment. Over time, this journaling practice reveals underlying patterns, helping the seeker understand and release energy held within each chakra. By addressing these deeper layers, the seeker experiences a release that goes beyond the surface, fostering a sense of freedom and lightness in the energy field.

To enhance spiritual clarity, Metatron introduces the use of "guided visualization for chakra clearing," a method that combines imagination with Metatron's healing light. In a meditative state, the seeker envisions each chakra as a beautiful, radiant flower—its color vibrant, its petals open, and its energy flowing freely. Starting at the root, the seeker visualizes Metatron's light pouring over each flower, gently washing away any dust or blockages that may have gathered. As the visualization progresses, each chakra flower feels fully open, vibrant, and alive, symbolizing the clearing of energetic impurities. This visualization practice strengthens the seeker's mental focus and allows them to connect with each chakra as a living, dynamic part of their spiritual anatomy.

Metatron teaches the seeker the importance of integrating these cleansing practices into their daily routine. Small, consistent habits—such as a morning breathwork session, the use of essential oils, or a few minutes of visualization—help maintain an open and balanced energy flow. Metatron emphasizes that these practices do not have to be elaborate; even simple acts performed with intention can have profound effects on the seeker's energy body. Through this integration, chakra cleansing becomes not just a healing exercise but a regular, nurturing ritual that supports the seeker's spiritual evolution.

With Metatron's guidance, the seeker learns that chakra cleansing is not merely about removing blockages; it is an act of self-respect, a celebration of the soul's natural light. Through each practice, the seeker feels renewed, as if the channels of energy within have been reset to a state of clarity and openness. The seeker discovers that true cleansing brings a sense of peace and empowerment, an alignment with both their inner being and the universal energy that flows through all creation. Metatron's teachings imbue each moment with reverence, reminding the seeker that chakra cleansing is a sacred renewal—a path that brings the soul into alignment with the divine, where energy flows freely, vibrantly, and in perfect harmony with the universe.

Chapter 15
Energy Alignment

Archangel Metatron now reveals the importance of aligning the energies within the seeker, guiding them to a unified flow of vitality, peace, and strength that resonates through body, mind, and spirit. This alignment is a practice of harmonizing the chakras as a single, integrated system, allowing the seeker's energy to move freely and with purpose. As each chakra supports the others, an uninterrupted flow is created, enabling a state of balance and connection with higher consciousness. Metatron's presence illuminates this process, ensuring that the seeker experiences alignment as a path to clarity, centeredness, and spiritual wholeness.

Metatron begins by inviting the seeker to experience their energy field as a cohesive structure rather than separate centers of energy. The seeker is guided to visualize their chakras as part of a flowing river, where each chakra acts as a segment that supports the movement of energy along the entire length. Any blockages,

Building on the principles of energy alignment, Archangel Metatron introduces specific practices that support the continuous flow and unity of the chakras, creating a foundation of stability, harmony, and spiritual depth. These techniques allow the seeker to deepen their understanding of how each energy center interacts, enhancing overall balance and coherence. Metatron guides the seeker to embrace this alignment not only as an occasional practice but as a state of being that connects them to the universe's rhythms and to the sacred essence within.

Metatron begins with the practice of "energy synchronization through breath," a technique that connects all the chakras with each inhale and exhale, reinforcing their unity. The seeker is guided to sit comfortably, breathing deeply while focusing on the entire chakra system. Starting from the root and moving upwards to the crown, the seeker visualizes a single stream of light, flowing smoothly through each chakra. With each inhale, the seeker draws energy upward; with each exhale, they send it downward, creating a balanced loop that integrates each chakra's unique qualities. Metatron's light strengthens this energy loop, ensuring that the seeker experiences a sense of calm and wholeness, as if their entire being is in harmonious flow.

Metatron then introduces "grounding and centering through visualization," a practice that anchors the seeker's energy field to both the earth and divine realms. In this exercise, the seeker imagines roots extending from the root chakra deep into the earth, absorbing the grounding energy of nature. Simultaneously, they visualize a stream of golden light descending from above, entering through the crown chakra and flowing downward. These energies meet at the heart chakra, merging into a radiant glow that pulses outward to all chakras. Metatron's presence amplifies this connection, helping the seeker feel both rooted and uplifted, a balance between earthly and spiritual energies that fosters a continuous, stable alignment.

To deepen this harmony, Metatron introduces "chakra weaving," an advanced visualization in which the seeker envisions threads of energy connecting each chakra to its neighboring centers. Starting at the root, the seeker imagines a thread of light weaving from the root to the sacral, then from the sacral to the solar plexus, and so on until they reach the crown. These threads are visualized as radiant, flexible lines that maintain a dynamic flow between each chakra. With Metatron's guidance, this weaving strengthens the connection between the chakras, transforming them from individual centers into a unified network. This practice encourages the seeker to feel each chakra's influence on the others, creating an interconnected system that resonates with vitality and strength.

Metatron also introduces "energy balancing with hand placement," a gentle practice of self-healing that uses the hands to balance and unify the chakra energy. The seeker is guided to place their hands on each chakra, starting at the root and moving upward. As they hold their hands over each center, they focus on feeling the energy flow between the chakras, allowing any imbalances to dissipate through gentle touch and intention. Metatron's energy surrounds the seeker's hands, amplifying their healing capacity and creating a sensation of warmth and calm. This hand placement practice serves as both a physical and spiritual gesture, one that aligns the seeker's energy in a nurturing and supportive way.

For moments when the seeker feels the need for rapid alignment, Metatron introduces the "one-breath alignment," a quick, centering technique that can be done anytime. With a deep inhale, the seeker visualizes energy entering through the crown and descending through each chakra in a single sweep. On the exhale, the energy flows down to the root and then returns upward, like a wave that refreshes each chakra simultaneously. Metatron's guidance allows this single breath to act as a powerful reset, instantly harmonizing the energy centers and providing a sense of renewed balance. This technique is particularly useful during times of stress or when the seeker feels out of alignment, providing an immediate way to reconnect with their centered self.

Metatron next introduces "energy bathing with light," a visualization technique in which the seeker imagines themselves immersed in a shower of light that cascades over their entire energy field. In a quiet space, the seeker envisions this light as a soft, golden flow that starts at the top of their head and moves downward, enveloping each chakra as it flows. The light acts as a cleansing and harmonizing force, dissolving any remaining density and leaving each chakra open and aligned. Metatron's presence enhances this experience, infusing the light with a healing quality that penetrates deeply into each chakra, creating a lasting sense of peace and integration. This light bath leaves the seeker feeling refreshed, as though their energy field has been renewed from within.

To support a deeper connection with their energy centers, Metatron encourages the seeker to keep a "chakra alignment journal," a personal record of alignment practices, insights, and sensations experienced during meditation. This journal serves as a reflective tool, allowing the seeker to note any shifts, patterns, or breakthroughs they observe over time. Through Metatron's guidance, each entry becomes a way to deepen awareness of how alignment influences their spiritual growth, revealing how the chakras work in unison to create balance and clarity. The act of journaling itself reinforces the practice, grounding the seeker's experience and helping them to see alignment as an ongoing journey.

Metatron concludes by reminding the seeker that energy alignment is not an end goal, but a practice of returning to one's natural state of flow. Through these advanced techniques, the seeker not only aligns their chakras but also aligns with the pulse of the universe itself. This harmonious flow empowers the seeker to move through life with greater clarity, compassion, and resilience. With each practice, the seeker comes to recognize that alignment is a state of attunement with their true self, a place of peace and strength that reflects the divine unity within.

Through Metatron's guidance, energy alignment becomes an act of devotion, an honoring of the self as a conduit for universal energy. The seeker learns that true alignment radiates from within, creating a state of harmony that connects them to the vast spiritual current that sustains and inspires all life. In this unity, the seeker walks forward grounded, centered, and illuminated, a being in alignment with the cosmos and the sacred flow of energy that guides their journey.

Chapter 16
Advanced Meditation

At this stage of the journey, Archangel Metatron introduces the seeker to advanced meditation techniques designed to deepen their connection with inner wisdom and access heightened states of awareness. Meditation, now more than a practice of stillness, becomes a gateway to profound self-knowledge and spiritual transcendence, leading the seeker closer to their true essence and to the divine presence within. With Metatron's guidance, these advanced techniques enable the seeker to tap into spiritual dimensions that reveal the vast potential for growth and illumination.

Metatron begins by introducing "mindful attunement," a practice of silent observation that invites the seeker to experience each sensation, thought, and feeling without judgment. This deep awareness extends beyond the physical, allowing the seeker to recognize the subtle energy shifts within their body. Through mindful attunement, the seeker notices how energy flows, where blockages or tensions may arise, and how each breath harmonizes the body and mind. Metatron's presence creates a gentle aura of support, helping the seeker feel grounded even as they explore these deeper layers. With each practice, the seeker becomes more attuned to their natural energy, learning to listen to the silent language of their being.

To deepen the seeker's meditative experience, Metatron introduces "visualization of the sacred light," a technique that enhances spiritual clarity. In this meditation, the seeker imagines a radiant sphere of light descending from above, entering through the crown chakra and filling the body with a sense of purity and warmth. This light, infused with Metatron's energy, moves slowly through each chakra, illuminating and harmonizing the inner landscape. As it reaches the heart, it expands outward, forming a shield of light around the seeker. This visualization not only fosters inner peace but also creates an energetic connection with higher realms, allowing the seeker to feel both protected and uplifted. Each meditation session leaves the seeker with a sense of clarity, as though their energy has been gently aligned with universal flow.

Metatron also teaches "mantra meditation," a powerful technique that uses sacred sounds to focus the mind and resonate with divine energy. The seeker chooses a mantra, a word or phrase that embodies spiritual truth, such as "Om" or "I am light." With each repetition, the mantra vibrates through the body, aligning the seeker's energy with the mantra's essence. Metatron guides the seeker to let go of distractions and merge fully with the sound, experiencing it as a continuous flow that connects their inner world with the infinite. Through regular practice, the seeker finds that the mantra acts as a bridge between thoughts and higher awareness, a sacred rhythm that grounds them in presence and opens them to new dimensions of consciousness.

For an even deeper connection, Metatron introduces "the practice of inner vision," where the seeker gently turns their awareness to the third eye, the energy center of insight and intuition located between the brows. Metatron guides the seeker to focus here, imagining a soft, indigo light that opens the mind to perceptions beyond the physical. In this state, the seeker may begin to perceive symbols, colors, or even messages that arise from within or from higher guidance. This technique enhances intuitive abilities, helping the seeker trust their inner wisdom and interpret the subtle language of the soul. Metatron's energy accompanies the seeker, ensuring that this exploration remains gentle, secure, and enriching. As the seeker practices inner vision, they cultivate a new level of spiritual perception, one that allows them to connect with universal truths in a direct and personal way.

Metatron also encourages the seeker to practice "grounded transcendence," a meditation that connects both earthly grounding and spiritual elevation. The seeker visualizes roots extending from the base of their spine deep into the earth, drawing up stabilizing energy that centers and nourishes them. Simultaneously, they imagine a beam of light ascending from the crown chakra, connecting them with divine wisdom. These dual currents of energy meet at the heart, blending into a radiant sphere of unity that allows the seeker to feel both rooted in the present moment and open to the infinite. Grounded transcendence teaches the seeker that spiritual exploration does not require separation from the physical world; rather, it reveals the spiritual within every aspect of existence. With Metatron's guidance, this meditation cultivates a balanced state of expansion and stability, helping the seeker move through daily life with both awareness and grounded peace.

In further guidance, Metatron introduces "observing the inner silence," a form of meditation that involves releasing all visualization and mantra, focusing solely on the silence within. This inner silence is not empty but alive, a space where the seeker can simply be, free from judgment or thought. In this state, the seeker may experience a profound sense of peace, where the boundaries of self and universe seem to dissolve. Metatron's energy surrounds this practice, helping the seeker feel held within this vast silence, a silence that reveals the depths of their spirit. With time, observing inner silence becomes a source of renewal, a place where the seeker can return to their essential self, untouched by external influences or inner chatter.

To enhance the benefits of these advanced techniques, Metatron suggests the seeker create a "sacred meditation space," a designated area filled with symbols, crystals, or objects that resonate with their spiritual path. This space becomes a sanctuary, a place where the seeker can focus inward without distraction. Metatron encourages the seeker to personalize this space with items that inspire peace, clarity, or connection, such as candles, incense, or a journal for reflections. Each object contributes to an environment that supports deep meditation, allowing the seeker to enter a state of openness and reverence each time they return. Over time, this space becomes a physical and energetic anchor, a reminder of the seeker's commitment to inner growth and alignment.

As the seeker becomes comfortable with these advanced practices, Metatron reminds them that meditation is a journey, not a destination. With each session, the seeker cultivates layers of awareness and depth, gradually awakening to the boundless potential of their inner world. Metatron's guidance infuses each technique with purpose and peace, helping the seeker to see meditation as more than an individual act but as a communion with universal consciousness. Through meditation, the seeker learns to touch the timeless essence within, experiencing life from a place of calm, insight, and connection.

With Metatron's support, these advanced meditation techniques offer the seeker a transformative experience, allowing them to navigate life with a sense of purpose and equanimity. Each practice becomes a way to explore and express the profound depths of the spirit, revealing the wisdom, light, and infinite peace that resides within. The seeker realizes that meditation is a path not only of self-discovery but of divine connection, a sacred journey that aligns them with the rhythm of the cosmos and the loving presence of Metatron, who guides them every step of the way.

With Metatron's guidance, the seeker is now prepared to deepen their meditation journey, exploring techniques that unlock profound spiritual experiences and expanded states of consciousness. These advanced practices refine their ability to connect to universal energies, enabling an intimate, transformative encounter with the higher realms. Each meditation leads the seeker beyond ordinary awareness, immersing them in the boundless peace and clarity that resides in pure presence.

Metatron introduces the seeker to "transcendent visualization," a technique that merges the power of imagination with divine guidance. In this meditation, the seeker envisions themselves standing in a landscape of light, surrounded by ethereal beauty that reflects the inner dimensions of their spirit. As they walk through this sacred space, each step becomes a journey inward, allowing them to sense Metatron's presence as a guide who opens new spiritual pathways. In this transcendent realm, the seeker may encounter symbols, colors, or even messages, each carrying meaning and insight for their journey. Metatron's energy illuminates the visualization, providing a radiant clarity that fills the seeker's heart with peace and purpose.

For those moments when the seeker seeks to experience deeper levels of serenity, Metatron introduces "breathing into stillness." This technique involves breathing in a rhythmic pattern that gradually slows down the body and mind, preparing them to enter a state of profound calm. The seeker inhales deeply, holds the breath for a moment, and then exhales slowly, releasing all tension with each breath. As they continue, they feel each part of their being soften and expand, entering a state where thoughts gently recede and stillness takes over. Within this stillness, Metatron's presence brings a sense of infinite space and time, a reminder that the soul's true nature is boundless. This practice reveals that inner silence is alive, a presence that radiates peace and deepens the seeker's connection with the sacred essence of all life.

Metatron next teaches "harmonic resonance," a meditation that uses specific frequencies to bring the seeker into alignment with the higher vibrations of divine consciousness. The seeker is guided to listen to or create sounds—such as soft hums or chimes—that resonate with each chakra, starting from the root and moving up to the crown. Each sound frequency aligns with the natural vibration of the chakra, cleansing and harmonizing it while inviting spiritual alignment. As the sounds resonate, Metatron's energy magnifies their effect, filling the seeker's entire being with waves of tranquility and oneness. This harmonic meditation brings the seeker's energy field into alignment with universal frequencies, allowing them to experience unity with all existence and to feel Metatron's loving presence in each vibration.

To explore consciousness beyond the physical form, Metatron introduces "expanded awareness," a meditation that opens the seeker to the vast realms of spiritual insight. The seeker begins by focusing on the space between their thoughts, observing the gaps of quiet that lie beneath mental activity. With each moment of stillness, they feel these spaces expand, dissolving the boundaries between self and the universe. Guided by Metatron, the seeker enters a field of awareness that extends beyond the body and into the essence of universal consciousness. Here, they experience a sensation of unity, where individual identity merges with a greater presence. This expanded awareness becomes a place of profound insight, where the seeker feels a deep knowing, as if they are in communion with the essence of existence itself.

In addition, Metatron introduces "light immersion," a meditation designed to heighten spiritual perception by immersing the seeker in pure light. The seeker visualizes themselves bathed in a radiant column of light that descends from the cosmos, illuminating every aspect of their being. This light is both gentle and powerful, cleansing any lingering density or resistance, creating an open and receptive state of mind. Under Metatron's guidance, the seeker merges with this light, experiencing it not as something external, but as their own essence—a reminder of their divine origin. This immersion in light expands the seeker's awareness and brings clarity to their journey, allowing them to feel aligned with the universal flow of life and with Metatron's energy.

To deepen the seeker's sensitivity to spiritual realms, Metatron introduces "mirror of the soul," a meditation that invites self-reflection and awareness of the soul's vastness. In this practice, the seeker envisions a clear, calm lake within which they see their reflection, representing both their inner and higher self. As they gaze into this mirror, they observe qualities, feelings, or images that surface—each reflection offering insight into their current spiritual state. Metatron's presence enhances the depth of this meditation, allowing the seeker to see not only their strengths but also areas for growth, gently guiding them toward inner understanding and acceptance. This soul mirror becomes a sacred tool, revealing aspects of the seeker's essence that are often hidden, and inviting them to embrace all facets of their being with compassion.

Metatron guides the seeker in "celestial alignment," a meditation that harmonizes their energy with cosmic forces and rhythms. In a quiet space, the seeker visualizes themselves connected to the movements of the stars, feeling the rhythm of the cosmos as a pulse within their own heart. They are guided to align their breathing and awareness with this universal rhythm, sensing how each breath connects them to the infinite cycles of life, death, and renewal. In this state of celestial harmony, the seeker feels Metatron's presence as a bridge between worlds, linking their human experience with the vast intelligence of the universe. This meditation provides a profound sense of purpose and belonging, as the seeker experiences their life as part of a greater cosmic dance, each moment aligned with the universe's unfolding.

Metatron reminds the seeker that these advanced meditation practices are tools for deep transformation, paths to an ever-greater sense of unity and self-discovery. Each meditation session, each journey into stillness, invites the seeker closer to the divine essence within. These techniques do not merely calm the mind; they open doorways to the soul, allowing the seeker to experience the divine within themselves and in all that surrounds them.

Through these advanced meditations, the seeker learns that spirituality is not a distant ideal but an intimate presence that permeates every aspect of existence. With each practice, the seeker grows closer to the mystery that lies within, finding in Metatron a guide who illuminates the path to true understanding. This journey becomes an ongoing dance of exploration, where every breath, every quiet moment, and every touch of inner silence reveals the boundless love and wisdom at the heart of the spiritual path.

Chapter 17
Chakras and Emotions

Metatron unveils the profound relationship between the chakras and human emotions, guiding the seeker to understand how each energy center holds, reflects, and responds to the emotional currents within. This connection is not merely symbolic but vibrational, with each chakra resonating with specific feelings and experiences, which in turn shape the seeker's sense of self, relationships, and overall spiritual well-being. Through Metatron's wisdom, the seeker learns that emotions are pathways to deeper self-knowledge and integral components of the spiritual journey.

Metatron introduces the root chakra, the foundation of security and survival, as the center where primal emotions—fear, trust, and safety—reside. Here, the seeker is invited to explore how feelings of stability or anxiety manifest in their physical world. Guided by Metatron, they reflect on how their relationship with security impacts their connection to others and their sense of grounding. This root chakra is like the earth itself, providing support but also storing unresolved fears. Metatron's energy surrounds this exploration, bringing a sense of peace and trust as the seeker looks within, releasing fears and renewing their sense of belonging.

The sacral chakra, the seat of creativity and desire, reveals the delicate interplay between passion and vulnerability. Metatron guides the seeker to connect with emotions such as joy, pleasure, and openness here, where the spirit engages in the dance of creation and relationships. The seeker reflects on how feelings of worthiness or inhibition may shape their creative expression and connections with others. This chakra resonates with a vibrant, flowing energy that invites release and renewal, encouraging the seeker to experience life fully. Metatron's presence enhances this exploration, helping the seeker to embrace both desire and self-acceptance, allowing them to feel the richness of life's experiences.

In the solar plexus, the chakra of personal power, Metatron directs the seeker's awareness to emotions of confidence, willpower, and self-worth. This center holds the strength to transform challenges and assert one's place in the world. Here, the seeker confronts feelings of inadequacy or pride, realizing how these energies influence their sense of autonomy. Under Metatron's guidance, the seeker visualizes this energy as a warm, golden light, expanding with each breath and dissolving any feelings of limitation. The solar plexus becomes a place of empowerment, where the seeker recognizes their ability to shape their path with courage and integrity, feeling supported by Metatron's strength.

With Metatron's guidance, the heart chakra reveals its role as the bridge between the physical and spiritual realms, embodying compassion, forgiveness, and love. Here, the seeker is invited to explore the depths of empathy and connection, understanding how feelings of love or resentment flow through this center. Metatron's energy embraces the heart chakra, allowing the seeker to feel safe as they open to vulnerability and healing. The seeker learns that the heart chakra is not only a place for personal emotions but a portal to universal love, where they can connect deeply with others and with their higher self, experiencing an expansive sense of unity.

At the throat chakra, the voice of truth and expression, Metatron guides the seeker to explore the emotions associated with communication and authenticity. This chakra reflects the harmony—or discord—between one's inner truth and outer expression. Here, Metatron encourages the seeker to recognize any feelings of suppression or empowerment, allowing them to speak their truth freely. As the seeker visualizes this center as a clear, blue energy, they feel Metatron's presence strengthening their voice, helping them to release any blocks to self-expression. The throat chakra becomes a channel for honesty and creativity, where the seeker learns to express their inner world with clarity and integrity.

Moving to the third eye, the center of intuition, Metatron illuminates the emotions tied to insight, perception, and clarity. This chakra invites the seeker to connect with their inner vision, feeling how intuition guides them beyond surface reality. Metatron encourages the seeker to observe emotions of doubt or faith that influence their ability to trust their own wisdom. Through meditation, the seeker visualizes the third eye as a soft indigo light, allowing Metatron's energy to bring clarity and insight. Here, the seeker transcends ordinary perception, connecting with deeper truths that enhance their spiritual understanding, learning that this chakra holds the potential to see beyond illusions.

The crown chakra represents the connection to the divine, a place where the seeker experiences a sense of transcendence and oneness. Emotions associated with this chakra are often subtle—feelings of peace, surrender, or bliss. Metatron's energy here is gentle yet expansive, guiding the seeker to let go of personal identity and merge with universal consciousness. The seeker visualizes a radiant violet light, feeling a profound connection to the cosmos and to the infinite wisdom that flows through them. In the crown chakra, they experience moments of pure being, an alignment with the divine that transcends all other emotions, leaving a sense of serenity and completeness.

Through each of these energy centers, Metatron reveals that emotions are not merely passing states but vital expressions of the soul's journey, resonating with each chakra's unique energy. The seeker comes to understand that emotions, rather than obstacles, are powerful guides, revealing areas of growth and opening doors to greater awareness. Metatron teaches that by acknowledging and honoring these emotional currents, the seeker aligns with their own truth, achieving a balance that brings harmony to both their inner and outer worlds.

This journey through the chakras and emotions becomes an exploration of self-compassion and acceptance, as the seeker learns to hold space for all facets of their emotional landscape. With Metatron's guidance, they recognize that emotions serve as both teachers and mirrors, reflecting the state of their energy centers and their connection with the divine. In each chakra, the seeker discovers a sacred opportunity to grow, heal, and deepen their relationship with themselves and the universe, realizing that emotions, like energy, are a dynamic, integral part of their spiritual essence.

As the seeker journeys deeper into the relationship between their chakras and emotions, Metatron introduces practices to release, heal, and harmonize emotional energy within each chakra. Emotions, when acknowledged and gently processed, act as catalysts for spiritual evolution, clearing energy channels and allowing for a more authentic connection with the self and the divine. Through these practices, the seeker learns how each chakra can become a sanctuary of peace and balance, free from the stagnation of past emotional burdens.

Metatron begins with the root chakra, where the seeker encounters the foundational feelings tied to survival, security, and belonging. Here, Metatron guides them to a grounding exercise designed to release deeply rooted fears. Visualizing roots extending from their feet into the earth, the seeker sends any unresolved anxieties downward, letting them dissipate into the soil. With each exhale, they feel lighter, supported by the earth's grounding energy. Metatron's presence reinforces the process, allowing the seeker to recognize and dissolve past fears that may have been locked in this chakra. As they complete the practice, the root chakra feels steadier, a secure base from which they can explore higher emotions and energies.

In the sacral chakra, the center of creativity and sensuality, Metatron leads the seeker through a "flow release" exercise. The seeker envisions water—a symbol of fluidity and emotion—

gently flowing through this chakra, cleansing away blockages tied to unexpressed emotions or suppressed desires. The water washes over any lingering feelings of guilt, shame, or hesitation, inviting the seeker to feel their own worthiness and creative potential. This practice, guided by Metatron, encourages a healthy release of emotions, transforming any stagnant energies into a renewed sense of joy and self-acceptance. The sacral chakra becomes a wellspring of inspiration, inviting the seeker to embrace life's pleasures and create freely.

Moving to the solar plexus, where personal power and confidence reside, Metatron introduces a "fire of transformation" visualization. Here, the seeker imagines a radiant fire at the center of their being, fueled by self-respect and courage. Any emotions of inadequacy, doubt, or anger are drawn into this fire, where they dissolve into warmth and light. The flame grows brighter with each breath, filling the seeker's core with empowerment and resilience. Metatron's guidance reinforces this inner strength, allowing the seeker to transform old patterns of self-doubt into a deep sense of personal integrity. This practice revitalizes the solar plexus, aligning it with the energy of purpose and action, ready to face challenges with courage and clarity.

At the heart chakra, Metatron guides the seeker through a practice of "compassionate release." Here, the seeker places a hand over their heart, breathing deeply and inviting any lingering feelings of grief, resentment, or heartache to rise gently to the surface. With Metatron's support, they envision these emotions as a soft mist, lifting from the heart and dispersing into the air. This release brings a profound sense of relief and lightness, allowing the heart chakra to open fully to compassion and love. The seeker learns to approach their emotions with kindness, realizing that every feeling—whether joyful or painful—has contributed to their journey. This compassionate release transforms the heart into a space of unity and acceptance, open to both giving and receiving love.

For the throat chakra, the center of truth and expression, Metatron introduces a "vocal release" exercise. The seeker is guided to speak or hum softly, allowing their voice to flow without constraint. This simple practice encourages them to release any emotions tied to unspoken truths or self-suppression. Through sound, the seeker lets go of the need to hide or control their feelings, experiencing the freedom of authentic expression. Metatron's presence amplifies this liberation, reminding the seeker that their voice is an instrument of truth. As they continue, the throat chakra clears, creating a channel for honest communication and creativity, a space where the seeker feels empowered to share their inner world with clarity.

At the third eye, the center of insight and intuition, Metatron leads the seeker through a "visionary release" exercise. Here, they close their eyes and allow any cloudy or unresolved emotions—such as confusion, doubt, or uncertainty—to gather as mist before their inner vision. With Metatron's guidance, the seeker visualizes a gentle light dissolving this mist, restoring clarity and enhancing intuition. This practice opens the third eye to clear perception, allowing the seeker to view their emotions from a place of wisdom rather than judgment. As the third eye chakra clears, the seeker becomes attuned to their inner guidance, seeing their emotional experiences as valuable insights that contribute to a broader understanding of their spiritual path.

At the crown chakra, Metatron introduces a "surrender and acceptance" practice. Here, the seeker visualizes their crown opening like a lotus, inviting divine light to fill their being. Any lingering emotional tension—feelings of separation, existential worry, or restlessness—gently rises from within, merging with the light above. This act of surrender is not one of giving up, but of releasing control and trusting in a higher purpose. Metatron's presence infuses this experience with serenity, as the seeker feels an expansive peace that surpasses all understanding. The crown chakra aligns with a profound sense of unity, as the seeker surrenders personal burdens and embraces the infinite support of the universe.

With each of these practices, the seeker not only releases emotional density but also learns to honor and integrate their emotional landscape as part of their spiritual journey. Metatron's teachings reveal that emotions, rather than obstacles, are gifts—guides that reveal where healing, growth, and alignment are needed. The seeker discovers that every chakra holds the potential for transformation, a space where emotions can be felt, acknowledged, and then released, creating a sense of balance that resonates through body, mind, and spirit.

As these practices become part of the seeker's routine, the chakras transform into sanctuaries of emotional and energetic harmony. The seeker realizes that this journey through emotions is one of self-compassion, a continuous practice of acknowledging, embracing, and ultimately releasing the energies that arise within. Metatron's guidance provides strength and solace, leading the seeker to see their emotions as sacred experiences that connect them to their humanity, their spirit, and the divine essence that unites all things. Through this deepened understanding, the seeker learns to live with an open heart, a clear mind, and a balanced soul, aligned with the universal flow of love and wisdom.

Chapter 18
Dream Work

The journey into dream work begins as Metatron guides the seeker to understand the power and significance of dreams in the realm of spiritual growth. Dreams are not random illusions of the mind but portals to the subconscious, revealing truths that may elude waking awareness. In these nighttime journeys, Metatron acts as a guardian and guide, illuminating the mysteries within, where the veil between the earthly and spiritual realms thins. Through the dream state, the seeker connects with their deepest intuitions, explores unresolved emotions, and receives messages from the divine.

Metatron introduces the seeker to the concept of the "dream space" as a sacred arena for soul exploration. This space, unrestricted by physical laws, allows the soul to travel, to experience, and to communicate without the confines of earthly form. In the dream realm, symbols and archetypes emerge, reflecting both the universal and individual aspects of consciousness. Metatron's guidance helps the seeker understand that each symbol or experience within a dream is meaningful, carrying messages that resonate deeply with their soul's journey.

To begin the practice of dream work, Metatron encourages the seeker to set intentions before sleep, creating a ritual that invites clarity and receptivity. Before resting, the seeker is guided to sit quietly, connecting with Metatron's energy and asking for insights to be revealed during their dreams. This intentional practice not only prepares the mind but also aligns the spirit with the intention of receiving guidance. By inviting Metatron into the dream space, the seeker establishes a spiritual safeguard and opens a pathway for wisdom to emerge.

Metatron teaches the seeker about common dream symbols, helping them recognize patterns that may surface repeatedly. A tree, for example, may symbolize growth, grounding, or family connections, depending on the dreamer's personal resonance with the image. Water can represent the fluid nature of emotions or the depths of the subconscious. Metatron's guidance allows the seeker to move beyond literal interpretations, showing them that symbols are reflections of their inner landscape. Through this understanding, each dream element becomes a part of a larger spiritual dialogue, a language through which the soul communicates.

As part of the dream work practice, Metatron introduces the seeker to the technique of dream journaling. Upon waking, the seeker is encouraged to immediately record their dreams, capturing details, emotions, and symbols before they fade. This practice allows for a gradual unfolding of meaning, as patterns and recurring themes emerge over time. By keeping a journal, the seeker can revisit and interpret dreams with greater clarity, recognizing how each dream intertwines with their spiritual journey. Metatron's presence supports this process, helping the seeker discern the layers of wisdom embedded in their dreams.

To deepen the practice, Metatron guides the seeker in understanding "lucid dreaming," a state where they become aware of dreaming while still within the dream. In this heightened state of awareness, the seeker can interact consciously with the dream environment, exploring the realms of their subconscious with intent and curiosity. Metatron's energy provides a protective presence, empowering the seeker to ask questions, seek guidance, or transform their experiences within the dream. Lucid dreaming allows for a profound level of self-discovery, as the seeker actively participates in their spiritual growth while bridging the conscious and subconscious mind.

Metatron also emphasizes the importance of paying attention to "recurring dreams" or "nightmares." These intense or repetitive dreams often highlight unresolved fears, traumas, or emotions that linger within the subconscious. Rather than viewing nightmares as disturbing, Metatron guides the seeker to see them as invitations to confront and release hidden fears. With his support, the seeker learns to approach these dreams with curiosity rather than avoidance, recognizing that each challenging dream holds an opportunity for healing and transformation. By facing these aspects of their inner world, the seeker integrates shadows into light, finding strength and clarity in the process.

As the seeker continues their dream practice, Metatron introduces them to "guided dreaming," a gentle method of asking specific questions or setting intentions to receive answers through dreams. This technique requires clarity and focus, as the seeker formulates a question or area of inquiry before sleep. With Metatron's guidance, they establish a sacred space of openness, allowing the dream realm to reveal insights and guidance. The seeker might seek clarity on life purpose, guidance on a relationship, or understanding of a personal challenge. Through this directed intention, dreams become a source of profound wisdom, guiding the seeker's actions and reflections in waking life.

Metatron encourages the seeker to view dreams as a way to connect with their higher self and the divine. Beyond symbols and insights, dreams can offer glimpses of other dimensions, past lives, or spiritual truths that transcend ordinary experience. The seeker learns to embrace dreams as sacred experiences, moments where they touch the realms of spirit and connect with the infinite. In these journeys, they may encounter spiritual guides, loved ones who have passed, or even memories that reach beyond this lifetime. Metatron's presence in these dreams provides a comforting sense of continuity and purpose, allowing the seeker to feel the divine connection that underlies their existence.

Through the practices of intention, journaling, interpretation, and guided dreaming, Metatron teaches that dreams are far more than passing shadows of the night—they are pathways to inner wisdom, healing, and spiritual expansion. Each dream becomes part of the seeker's journey, a mirror that reflects both their inner struggles and their spiritual progress. With Metatron's support, the seeker learns to navigate the dream space as a realm of possibility and insight, a place where the soul's voice speaks clearly, guiding them toward their highest potential.

In understanding and embracing dream work, the seeker discovers a deeper connection to their inner self and a profound trust in the guidance of the universe. Through each dream, the seeker steps closer to understanding the mysteries within, where every night's journey brings new insights, illuminations, and a sense of communion with the divine.

With Metatron's guidance, the seeker now embarks on deepening their dream work practice, transforming dreams into a sacred tool for ongoing spiritual development. These nighttime journeys become a conscious process, inviting divine insight, healing, and self-realization. Metatron's presence within these practices acts as a protective light, guiding the seeker to engage with dreams more intentionally, revealing truths that may be hidden during waking hours.

One of the key techniques Metatron introduces is the practice of "dream journaling with intention." In this practice, the seeker, before sleep, sets a specific intention for what they wish to learn, heal, or explore within their dreams. Metatron guides them to choose a question or area of focus, such as a relationship challenge, a life decision, or an aspect of self-growth. With this intention set, the seeker writes it clearly in their journal before bed, reinforcing their openness to receive guidance. By forming this intention, the dream state aligns with the seeker's focused energy, offering messages that speak directly to their inner questions.

Upon waking, Metatron encourages the seeker to capture the dream's details immediately—symbols, emotions, colors, or any lingering impressions. Even fragments hold meaning, and over time, patterns begin to emerge. This cumulative journal of dreams becomes a wellspring of guidance, revealing not only answers to specific questions but also broader themes and lessons woven throughout the seeker's spiritual journey. With Metatron's support, the seeker comes to see the dream journal as a dialogue between their conscious mind and the soul, each entry an unfolding map of their inner world.

To deepen the insight gained from each dream, Metatron introduces "symbol meditation." After recording a dream, the seeker selects one symbol that stood out—a place, a person, an object, or even a color—and meditates on it. With eyes closed, they visualize this symbol, holding it gently in their mind, and allowing any associated feelings or memories to surface. Under Metatron's guidance, the seeker uncovers layers of meaning, as the symbol may carry personal, archetypal, or spiritual resonance. This process reveals how a single symbol can act as a bridge between the subconscious and the divine, illuminating hidden aspects of the self.

Metatron also introduces the practice of "pre-sleep ritual," where the seeker creates a sacred space each night to prepare for conscious dreaming. By lighting a candle, playing soft music, or simply sitting in quiet reflection, the seeker signals a willingness to receive wisdom from the dream realm. This ritual becomes a gateway, helping the seeker transition from the busyness of waking life into a receptive, peaceful state. With Metatron's protective presence, they feel a sense of safety as they enter the dream world, knowing they are surrounded by a light that allows them to journey without fear. Through this ritual, each night's sleep becomes a sacred act, an invitation to explore the realms of the subconscious and divine.

Lucid dreaming, where the seeker becomes aware of dreaming while still within the dream, is another practice Metatron supports. By becoming conscious in their dreams, the seeker can explore specific questions, interact with symbols, or confront any fears in real-time. Metatron's energy helps stabilize this awareness, allowing the seeker to observe and engage with their dreams intentionally. This technique transforms the dream world into a canvas for growth and exploration, where the seeker can actively participate in their spiritual evolution. Metatron teaches that lucid dreams are not only for curiosity but serve as powerful tools for self-transformation, as they offer a direct pathway to face and release inner blocks.

For those dreams that stir unease or distress, Metatron introduces the "healing the shadow" technique. Some dreams reveal unresolved fears or suppressed emotions, which appear as shadows in the dream world. With Metatron's guidance, the seeker learns to approach these challenging dreams with compassion and courage, seeing them as opportunities to embrace and heal parts of themselves. Upon waking, the seeker is encouraged to write down the dream and reflect on any emotional responses it stirred. They then visualize Metatron's healing light enveloping the shadow aspects within the dream, transforming fear or discomfort into acceptance and understanding. This practice allows the seeker to integrate aspects of themselves that may have been ignored or hidden, fostering inner wholeness.

Metatron teaches the seeker the art of "divine inquiry." In this advanced practice, the seeker requests insight or guidance from Metatron or other spiritual guides within the dream state. Before sleep, they hold a question in their mind or write it down, asking for clarity on matters of purpose, spiritual growth, or guidance through life's uncertainties. With Metatron's support, the dream space becomes a sanctuary for divine messages, where wisdom flows freely and unfiltered. These inquiries may result in dreams where symbolic answers are presented, or they may open the seeker to subtle impressions upon waking. Over time, the seeker builds a relationship with their inner guidance, learning to trust the messages that come through, both during dreams and in their waking life.

As the seeker deepens these practices, Metatron reveals that the dream realm serves not only as a space for personal insight but also as a link to the universal consciousness that connects all beings. Through dreams, the seeker taps into a collective wisdom, where their own experiences resonate with the archetypal stories and symbols shared across humanity. This realization brings a sense of unity and belonging, as the seeker understands that their dreams are a part of a larger tapestry of spiritual experiences, woven with the lives and lessons of many souls.

With Metatron's guidance, the seeker comes to view their dreams as a divine gift, a nightly ritual of self-discovery and connection to the infinite. Dreams are no longer fleeting visions but purposeful messages, each one a step on the path toward greater wisdom and self-understanding. By embracing dream work, the seeker cultivates a lifelong practice of listening, learning, and integrating the deeper truths revealed within the sacred space of dreams. Through each night's journey, they strengthen their bond with Metatron, experiencing dreams as a profound and sacred dialogue between their soul and the divine.

Chapter 19
Action and Karma

In the dance of existence, each action carries a thread of energy, reverberating across time and space, binding one moment to the next. Here, the profound essence of karma unfolds—the spiritual law of cause and effect—which teaches that every thought, intention, and action molds the path one walks. Guided by Metatron, the seeker is called to recognize how every decision, whether made consciously or unconsciously, shapes the spirit's journey, paving the way for growth or entanglement.

As the seeker gazes upon karma, Metatron illuminates it as a teacher, not a punishment or reward, but a mirror reflecting the lessons necessary for spiritual evolution. Metatron's light uncovers how each action holds the power to either harmonize or disrupt one's inner alignment. The seeker learns that karma is not bound by simplistic ideas of good or bad, but rather is woven through the tapestry of intention. In aligning actions with pure intent, the seeker can elevate their karmic path, redirecting energy toward harmony and growth. It is here that Metatron becomes not only a guide but a guardian of balance, showing how to release patterns that no longer serve and to cultivate those that uplift the soul.

One of the fundamental practices Metatron offers is the "Karmic Reflection Meditation." In this meditative state, the seeker is encouraged to review recent actions and interactions, allowing awareness to bring forth insights into the energies each action has set into motion. In this silent communion, Metatron invites the seeker to observe without judgment, gently unveiling patterns or intentions that need healing. Here, the seeker reflects on whether their actions emerge from love, compassion, and unity, or from fear, resentment, or self-centeredness. This meditation becomes a sacred space for transformation, as the seeker learns to realign their intent with spiritual values, letting go of actions that disrupt inner peace.

Metatron also introduces the practice of "Karmic Intent Setting." Each morning, before the day's activities unfold, the seeker sits in stillness and calls forth Metatron's guidance to set intentions that resonate with their highest self. By consciously establishing these intentions, the seeker infuses their actions with purpose and alignment, transforming daily activities into mindful expressions of their spiritual journey. Intentions may include kindness, honesty, patience, or other virtues, chosen to guide the day's encounters. Through this practice, Metatron shows the seeker that karma is not only a response to past actions but an opportunity to shape the present, empowering the seeker to weave a life rooted in alignment and truth.

Within the realm of karma, the law of action intersects with forgiveness, and here, Metatron's teachings guide the seeker toward liberation from past missteps. Through the "Forgiveness Ritual," the seeker learns that forgiveness is a potent means of releasing karma. Guided by Metatron, they identify any lingering resentment or guilt tied to past actions, whether directed toward others or oneself. In this ritual, they visualize Metatron's light encompassing these feelings, dissolving them into understanding and compassion. As forgiveness takes root, a release occurs, freeing the seeker from karmic bonds that might otherwise weigh down the spirit. Metatron teaches that through genuine forgiveness, the seeker not only finds peace but also purifies their karmic path, unburdened by past shadows.

Moreover, Metatron reveals the importance of "Karmic Service," a practice of balancing one's energy by offering kindness and support to others. By engaging in acts of selfless service—be it offering time, resources, or even a compassionate word—the seeker plants seeds of positive karma. Metatron emphasizes that true service arises from the heart, expecting no reward, and by serving in this spirit, the seeker generates vibrations of harmony that extend beyond the self. Each act of service resonates through the spiritual realms, contributing to the collective upliftment of consciousness. In this way, Metatron shows that karma is not isolated to individual growth but is interwoven with the growth of all beings, reminding the seeker that their journey is inherently tied to the collective whole.

To deepen this understanding, Metatron introduces the seeker to the "Wheel of Karma" visualization. In this practice, the seeker envisions karma as a great, turning wheel, each spoke representing an action or decision from their life. Metatron guides them to recognize that while the wheel turns continuously, they possess the power to influence its direction. By choosing actions aligned with love, honesty, and compassion, the seeker alters the wheel's momentum, steering it toward harmony. This visualization instills a sense of responsibility, as the seeker understands that every thought and choice contributes to the wheel's path, illustrating the interconnected nature of all actions.

Metatron teaches the seeker about "Mindful Choice," a practice where, before making significant decisions, they pause to consider the karmic implications. In these moments, Metatron's wisdom flows through, encouraging the seeker to weigh their actions in the balance of spiritual growth. This practice cultivates patience and discernment, helping the seeker make choices that not only fulfill immediate desires but also align with their higher self. Through Mindful Choice, the seeker realizes that the smallest decisions—how they respond to others, where they invest their time—are opportunities to create positive karma. This mindful awareness fosters a life of intentionality, where actions resonate with the seeker's purpose, contributing to an ongoing journey of spiritual evolution.

Under Metatron's guidance, karma emerges not as a distant cosmic force, but as a deeply personal and transformative process. Each action, no matter how simple, becomes a brushstroke on the canvas of the soul, shaping the unfolding masterpiece of one's life. With newfound clarity, the seeker steps forward, empowered by the understanding that they are the artist of their own karma, capable of creating a path that honors the soul's highest calling. Metatron's teachings illuminate this truth: that karma, when approached with awareness and love, becomes a compass guiding the seeker toward spiritual freedom, wisdom, and harmony.

With an awakened understanding of karma, the seeker is now led deeper into the intricacies of transformation. Metatron reveals that karma, when consciously engaged with, becomes a potent source of freedom, allowing the soul to transcend past limitations and create a life imbued with purpose. Through practices that dissolve old karmic patterns and establish new ones, the seeker embarks on a journey of purification, harmonizing actions with the soul's highest intentions.

At the heart of this transformation is the "Karmic Release Ritual," a practice that Metatron shares to guide the seeker in releasing burdens from past lives and unresolved patterns of this lifetime. In a space of solitude, the seeker enters a state of deep meditation, visualizing Metatron's radiant light enveloping them. With each exhalation, they release layers of past decisions and actions that may have been misaligned with love and truth. The seeker becomes aware that these patterns are not fixed; they are malleable, awaiting the seeker's conscious effort to transform them. Metatron's presence infuses this ritual with power, offering both liberation from the karmic weight and a profound sense of forgiveness, encouraging the seeker to accept and love the self beyond its past actions.

The seeker is also introduced to the "Mirror of Truth" meditation, a reflective practice that brings clarity to the areas of life where karma manifests most strongly. Through this meditation, the seeker sits before an imagined mirror in their mind's eye, where Metatron's guiding presence encourages them to gaze at their reflections with courage. Here, the seeker begins to recognize patterns in relationships, choices, or recurring challenges, seeing how certain karmic threads have woven through their life's tapestry. This awareness allows the seeker to identify the core lessons they have come to learn, moving from unconscious repetition to conscious transformation. In the Mirror of Truth, the seeker sees not only where healing is needed but also where progress has been made, inspiring confidence in the path ahead.

With a deepened understanding, Metatron introduces the practice of "Karmic Reconciliation." In this sacred act, the seeker reaches out, spiritually or physically, to individuals with whom karmic ties require healing. Whether through heartfelt conversations, written words, or simply a meditative intention, the seeker extends forgiveness and seeks to restore harmony. Metatron teaches that this act of reconciliation, even if done in spirit, has the power to dissolve karmic knots, releasing energies tied to unresolved emotions. As these connections are mended, the seeker's spirit is freed, creating space for more aligned and harmonious relationships.

Beyond reconciliation, Metatron guides the seeker toward the "Practice of Intentional Virtue." By consciously choosing virtues such as kindness, honesty, and humility, the seeker actively sows the seeds of positive karma. Each interaction becomes an opportunity to affirm these qualities, which create ripples of elevated energy. Through intentional virtue, the seeker reshapes their karmic landscape, understanding that each action not only impacts their immediate environment but reverberates within the spiritual realms. Metatron's wisdom reveals that such practice of virtue is not about perfection but about sincere intention, which is ultimately what transforms karma into a path of grace.

Additionally, Metatron introduces the "Karmic Writing Exercise," a practice where the seeker takes time to record reflections on recent actions, choices, and feelings. With a journal in hand, the seeker reflects on daily interactions, recording where they felt aligned with their higher self and where they may have acted out of alignment. Metatron encourages an honest, nonjudgmental approach to this writing, fostering awareness rather than guilt. Through this practice, the seeker gains insight into the subtle ways karma shapes each day, gradually refining actions to resonate with their spiritual path. In this process of reflection, the seeker transforms unexamined habits into conscious acts of love and compassion.

To further reinforce karmic release, Metatron introduces the seeker to the power of "Sacred Chanting," using specific mantras that are known to purify karma on a vibrational level. Each mantra, when intoned with intention, dissolves accumulated energetic residues, bringing a sense of lightness and renewal. Through the rhythmic repetition of sound, the seeker becomes attuned to frequencies that harmonize the spirit, allowing for the release of dense, stagnant energies. Metatron's guidance illuminates the potency of these ancient sounds, reminding the seeker that vibrational alignment through chanting connects them with the divine flow, dissolving past actions in a sea of universal love and forgiveness.

In the closing practices of karmic alignment, Metatron teaches the seeker about "Future Karma Creation," a proactive approach to set intentions that align with the soul's purpose. By visualizing the actions, relationships, and achievements they aspire to cultivate, the seeker consciously directs energy into creating a future filled with integrity, kindness, and purpose. Metatron's presence in this visualization imbues it with clarity, guiding the seeker to imagine a life path that echoes their truest values. This act of envisioning becomes an energetic blueprint, planting seeds for positive karma in the days and years to come. Future Karma Creation aligns the seeker with a path of conscious manifestation, transforming them into an active co-creator of their spiritual destiny.

With each of these practices, the seeker's understanding of karma deepens, transcending simplistic notions of cause and effect to embrace karma as a dynamic relationship with the universe. The actions they once performed unconsciously become opportunities for spiritual expression, as they align their intent with Metatron's teachings. Through this alignment, the seeker's journey transforms from one of reaction to one of creation, where each step is a conscious choice in service of their higher self.

In Metatron's light, the seeker finds not only the path to karmic liberation but also the realization that karma, when purified and consciously directed, reveals the essence of true freedom. The soul, having unburdened itself from patterns of the past, moves forward with lightness, wisdom, and unwavering purpose, united with the infinite dance of the divine.

Chapter 20
Spiritual Realization

The journey toward spiritual realization begins with an inward turn, a quiet return to the depths of one's essence, where the soul and the divine meet. In the subtle realms of inner silence, Archangel Metatron beckons the seeker to a transformative process—one that moves beyond knowledge or ritual and into the realm of profound presence. Here, in this space between thought and spirit, lies the essence of spiritual realization, a state where the individual soul awakens to its timeless nature, its connection to the vast consciousness that underlies all of existence.

Metatron's guidance brings the seeker to a place of inner clarity, helping them understand that spiritual realization is neither an arrival nor an achievement, but a continuous state of being. Through patient practice and surrender, the seeker learns to release attachments that bind the soul to transient concerns, embracing instead a path illuminated by the quiet joy of inner freedom. Metatron's voice, like a soft light, reveals the truth that spiritual realization is an unfolding process, a gradual removal of the veils that obscure the pure, unfiltered self.

Metatron introduces the "Awakening of Presence" meditation, a practice designed to cultivate a deep state of awareness beyond the churning mind. Here, the seeker learns to sit in stillness, to observe thoughts without attachment, to watch emotions without reaction. This practice of presence reveals the soul's essence as an unwavering point of consciousness. Through the discipline of silence, the seeker becomes acquainted with the subtle language of the spirit, attuning to the quiet vibrations of wisdom that arise within. Each session strengthens the soul's capacity to remain anchored in the present moment, untouched by the external world's fluctuations. In this sacred stillness, Metatron's light becomes a guiding beacon, inviting the seeker into ever-deeper communion with their higher self.

To further nurture this connection, Metatron introduces the concept of "Heart-Mind Unification," a practice that aligns intellect with intuition. Here, the seeker places one hand over the heart, feeling the rhythmic beat, while the other hand rests on the third eye, connecting the mind with the heart's wisdom. Through breathing exercises and mindful alignment, the seeker harmonizes the intellect's focus with the heart's inner knowing, bridging the gap between thought and feeling. This integration becomes a pathway to spiritual clarity, where decisions and insights emerge not from isolated reasoning, but from a deep, unified sense of truth and compassion.

Metatron also introduces the practice of "Soul Contemplation," a gentle exploration of one's eternal essence beyond personal identity. In a quiet space, the seeker contemplates the vast journey of the soul, visualizing its travels across lifetimes, its growth, and the wisdom it has gathered. Guided by Metatron's light, the seeker glimpses the soul's transcendence beyond physical life, understanding themselves not as a single lifetime but as an unfolding consciousness, evolving toward divine unity. This contemplation allows the seeker to release the ego's narrow perspective, recognizing that spiritual realization extends beyond the self and encompasses the entirety of existence.

As this deepened awareness unfolds, Metatron guides the seeker into the "Path of Surrender," a process of gently releasing control and allowing the divine to flow through each moment. The seeker learns to trust in the wisdom of the universe, letting go of the need to dictate outcomes or cling to specific desires. Metatron teaches that true surrender is not passive, but rather an active alignment with the highest energies, an invitation for the divine to move freely within the soul. Through this surrender, the seeker becomes an instrument of divine presence, experiencing the peace and harmony that arise when the self rests fully in universal flow.

In this state of surrender, Metatron introduces the "Breath of Divine Union," a breathing practice that unites the self with the expansive field of cosmic consciousness. The seeker inhales with the intention of drawing in divine energy, visualizing each breath as a wave of light entering the body. With each exhale, they release the boundaries of the self, dissolving into the vastness of the universe. This rhythm of inhalation and exhalation becomes a dance with the divine, where the seeker transcends individual awareness and merges with the limitless presence of the cosmos. Each breath reinforces the experience of interconnectedness, drawing the seeker into the profound peace that accompanies the realization of unity with all.

Metatron's guidance also emphasizes the "Witness State," where the seeker cultivates the ability to observe life from a detached perspective. In this state, they learn to watch their own actions, thoughts, and feelings without judgment, as though observing a river flowing past. This witnessing becomes a powerful tool in dissolving the ego's grip, creating a space where the soul's essence shines forth unobstructed. Through the witness state, the seeker experiences life as a sequence of experiences flowing in and out of awareness, realizing that their true self remains unchanged—a silent witness to all.

Metatron then introduces the "Light of Compassion" meditation, in which the seeker is guided to embody an open-hearted compassion for all beings. As they sit in meditation, they imagine Metatron's light expanding from their heart, encompassing everyone in their life, extending outward to all beings, and touching every soul. This light of compassion opens a channel within, allowing the seeker to experience a profound empathy that goes beyond individual identity. Through this expansion of compassion, the seeker touches the essence of divine love, realizing that at the heart of spiritual realization lies a boundless, inclusive love that embraces all of creation.

In closing, Metatron reveals that spiritual realization is the ultimate gift of the soul's journey. It is the understanding that one is a spark of the divine, a part of the endless unfolding of consciousness. With each moment of presence, each act of compassion, and each breath of surrender, the seeker steps closer to the truth of their infinite nature. This realization brings a profound sense of peace, for in recognizing themselves as a manifestation of divine light, the seeker discovers that they have always been whole, always connected, and eternally at one with the vastness of creation.

In the silent depths of spiritual realization, a stillness emerges, carrying with it the weightless resonance of the divine. As the seeker continues to peel back layers of self-illusion, Metatron's presence guides them toward a profound encounter with the true essence, the inner light of consciousness that exists unbound by space or time. This deepens the seeker's journey, refining their practice to achieve a state of unified awareness where the boundaries between self and the universe dissolve.

Metatron begins by inviting the seeker to explore the "Sanctuary of Inner Silence," a meditative practice that cultivates the quiet mind. Within this sanctuary, thoughts are observed, acknowledged, and then gently released, allowing the seeker to drift into a place beyond thought—a vast, spacious awareness. It is in this silence that the most profound truths are revealed, not through words but through direct experience. Here, the seeker learns to dwell in the unspoken wisdom of the soul, understanding that each moment of pure presence is a moment of communion with the divine. Through sustained practice, this state of silence becomes a refuge, a wellspring of insight and serenity that continues to expand with each visit.

In this state of silent awareness, Metatron introduces "The Light of Self-Recognition." This practice encourages the seeker to confront and embrace their own divinity, to look inward and recognize themselves as a fragment of the eternal, woven from the same threads as the cosmos. Through visualization, the seeker envisions a brilliant, unending light within, a beacon that connects them to the infinite. This light becomes a guide, reminding them of their inherent divinity, and dissolving the layers of ego that obscure true spiritual vision. Metatron's presence becomes a quiet witness to this realization, guiding the seeker toward a deeper acceptance of their divine nature and the understanding that, at the core, all beings share this radiant essence.

To deepen this awareness, Metatron introduces the "Practice of Radiant Love." This practice calls for the seeker to visualize the inner light extending outward, enveloping not only their own being but expanding to touch all of existence. As the light of love flows, the seeker becomes a conduit for universal love, dissolving any lingering barriers between themselves and others. Metatron emphasizes that this act of love is not merely emotional but is a recognition of the oneness of all things. It is through this radiant love that the seeker transcends individual perspective, realizing that in truth, there is no separation between souls; all are parts of the same divine whole.

With each step toward spiritual realization, Metatron reveals another layer of inner wisdom, guiding the seeker through the "Union of Breath and Spirit." In this exercise, breathing becomes an act of worship, each breath an acknowledgment of divine energy filling the body and soul. The seeker inhales deeply, visualizing the breath as pure energy entering the body, and exhales with the intent to merge with the cosmos. Each inhalation pulls in divine life, while each exhalation releases attachment, dissolving the self into the all-encompassing essence of the universe. Over time, this practice awakens the experience of unity, as if the seeker were a single wave upon an infinite ocean, both distinct and one with the whole.

Metatron introduces "The Mirror of Inner Truth," a meditative practice that brings forth clarity in recognizing and embracing the entirety of one's journey, including the shadows that lie within. By gazing inward without judgment, the seeker is invited to accept every facet of their being. This mirror reveals both the light and shadow, encouraging an embrace of all aspects of the self. It is through this unconditional self-acceptance that the seeker understands that the divine is present in all experiences—each moment, each challenge, and each joy. The inner mirror becomes a gateway to a higher truth: that spiritual realization is not the absence of flaws, but the integration of all facets into a harmonious whole.

In this state of harmony, Metatron introduces "The Flow of Divine Consciousness." This is the practice of surrendering completely to the flow of life, allowing each experience to unfold without resistance. Here, the seeker lets go of the need to control or shape events, stepping back to witness the divine hand at work. In surrendering to this flow, the seeker enters a dance with the universe, a dynamic exchange where every moment is both guided by divine intention and filled with spiritual purpose. The experience of life becomes a seamless integration of divine will and personal journey, where every action, thought, and feeling resonates with the energy of universal alignment.

Metatron then guides the seeker toward "The Sacred Return to Self." This practice takes the seeker back to the origin point of consciousness, a return to the unconditioned, untouched awareness present since the beginning of their spiritual path. Through a series of meditative visualizations, the seeker moves beyond the roles, identities, and experiences accumulated over time, arriving at the pure consciousness that remains after everything else falls away. This state of pure awareness is free from labels, fears, or attachments—it is simply the essence of being. Within this return, the seeker finds peace, and Metatron's presence is felt as a grounding force, a reminder that the spiritual journey has brought them full circle to a place of inner unity.

At the culmination of this journey, Metatron offers the practice of "Universal Embrace." In this final exercise, the seeker visualizes themselves as both an individual soul and part of the boundless universe. They feel their connection to the earth, the stars, and all living beings, recognizing that in spiritual realization, there is no beginning or end. This practice becomes a reminder that they are never alone, as they exist in a perpetual embrace with all that is. The sense of separation fades entirely, replaced by a profound knowing that they are an expression of divine love, interconnected with all that exists.

In the embrace of spiritual realization, the seeker's heart, mind, and soul merge with the divine flow, achieving a state of transcendent peace. The presence of Metatron fades into the background, a silent companion on a journey that has no final destination. The seeker comes to understand that true spiritual realization is a living, breathing experience—a continuous unfolding of awareness, an ever-deepening communion with the universe.

As they breathe in the truth of their divine nature, they realize that this journey is not one of becoming something new but of returning to what they have always been: a vessel of divine light, whole, infinite, and at one with the vast tapestry of existence. The path of spiritual realization remains open, ever-waiting, a limitless expanse where they are both an individual soul and the entirety of the cosmos intertwined.

Chapter 21
Manifestation

The final stretch of the spiritual journey with Metatron brings the seeker into the sacred art of manifestation. Here, the accumulated energy from aligned chakras, inner peace, and newfound wisdom begins to coalesce, forming a conduit through which intentions can take shape in both the spiritual and material worlds.

Metatron guides the seeker to the foundational principle of manifestation: "Clarity of Intention." This principle emphasizes that every thought, word, and feeling carries energy, and when aligned with purpose, this energy gains immense creative power. Clarity of intention is more than simply knowing what one desires; it involves cultivating a profound connection with one's innermost self to unearth desires that stem from the soul's purpose rather than the fleeting needs of the ego. The seeker learns to sit in stillness, asking themselves not just *what* they wish to create, but *why* this desire aligns with their spiritual journey. Metatron's guidance encourages an honest reflection, allowing the seeker to filter out desires rooted in illusion, anchoring their intentions in authenticity.

The seeker then engages in "The Circle of Alignment," a visualization that connects each intention with the energy of the chakras. In this practice, the seeker envisions their desire as a radiant sphere of light, suspended within the energy field. Each chakra is then visualized, lending its unique energy to the intention. The root chakra infuses stability and grounding; the sacral chakra adds creativity and emotional resonance; the solar plexus empowers the intention with will and confidence; the heart chakra imbues it with compassion; the throat chakra allows it to be expressed truthfully; the third eye grants insight and clarity, and the crown chakra opens the intention to divine guidance. Through this process, the seeker unifies body, mind, and spirit around their manifestation, creating an intention that is balanced, potent, and divinely aligned.

In guiding the seeker to this unity, Metatron introduces "The Breath of Manifestation." This exercise employs the breath as a channel to project intentions into the universe. The seeker is encouraged to take deep, deliberate breaths, visualizing each inhalation as drawing in divine energy to amplify their intention and each exhalation as releasing this intention into the cosmos. This rhythmic breathing serves as a reminder that manifestation is an ongoing dance of receptivity and release, of welcoming guidance and letting go. Through breath, the seeker not only enlivens the intention but also entrusts it to the divine flow, understanding that true manifestation arises from a blend of focused will and open surrender.

Metatron then leads the seeker into "The Light of Co-Creation," a practice that invites a partnership with the universe. Here, manifestation is seen not as an isolated act but as a collaborative endeavor, where the seeker recognizes that every intention set forth resonates within the web of existence. As they visualize their intention, the seeker imagines threads of light connecting them to all beings, as if each thought and action were a note in a cosmic symphony. In this awareness, they understand that their manifestations not only shape their own path but also ripple out, influencing the collective. This practice nurtures a sense of responsibility, guiding the seeker to focus on intentions that benefit not only themselves but the broader world.

"The Mirror of Trust" becomes another integral part of manifestation. Trust is the energy that sustains an intention as it moves through unseen realms before materializing in the physical. Here, Metatron encourages the seeker to gaze inward, contemplating the nature of their faith. Trust in the process, in their worthiness, and in the wisdom of divine timing all form a foundation upon which intentions are built. In quiet meditation, the seeker learns to recognize and release doubts, embracing an unwavering belief in the possibility and timing of their manifestations. Through the mirror of trust, the seeker understands that their role is not to question the how or when, but to remain steadfast in the conviction that what is meant to manifest will do so in its perfect time.

To deepen this understanding, Metatron introduces "The Seed of Divine Intent." In this visualization, the seeker is invited to imagine their intention as a seed planted within the vast garden of the universe. This seed is nurtured by the energies of love, patience, and gratitude. Just as a seed grows in darkness before emerging into light, the seeker learns that manifestations may develop beneath the surface, beyond immediate perception. Here, the practice of daily gratitude becomes a way of watering the seed, keeping the energy of intention alive without the strain of impatience or attachment. In honoring the unseen growth, the seeker recognizes that every intention, like a seed, requires time, space, and care to flourish.

Metatron then introduces the "Ritual of Aligned Action." While intention and visualization are powerful, action is the bridge that transforms energy into form. The seeker learns that action, when aligned with intention, amplifies the power of manifestation. In this ritual, they reflect on small, purposeful steps they can take each day to move closer to their goals. Metatron guides the seeker to see each action, no matter how seemingly insignificant, as a contribution to their manifestation. With each deliberate step, they honor the process of co-creation, blending their human efforts with divine intention to form a powerful current that propels their desires into reality.

The section concludes with "The Circle of Release," a final practice of letting go. Once the seeker has clarified their intention, aligned their energy, and taken aligned actions, Metatron encourages them to release their attachment to the outcome. In the circle of release, they visualize their intention rising upward, like a balloon lifted by the wind, carrying it into the boundless expanse of the cosmos. This act of release signifies a deep trust in the universe, an acknowledgment that they have done their part. Metatron's presence offers a gentle reminder that true manifestation is as much about surrender as it is about creation. In releasing the intention, the seeker opens the space for unexpected blessings and possibilities to flow in, allowing the manifestation to unfold in ways that serve the highest good.

The practice of final manifestation becomes a profound exercise in balance—holding the desire with intention, yet releasing it with trust; acting with purpose, yet surrendering attachment to the form it takes. In this sacred equilibrium, the seeker discovers that they are not merely a passive participant in life but a dynamic creator, weaving their energy into the fabric of existence.

As the seeker breathes in the fulfillment of their intentions, they realize that manifestation is not merely a means to an end but a transformative journey that shapes their character, refines their soul, and brings them ever closer to the divine. In the space between intention and realization, they encounter the mysteries of creation, the alchemy of spirit and matter, and the profound truth that every desire, when aligned with purpose, holds the potential to bridge heaven and earth.

In the final stage of manifestation, the seeker moves beyond individual practices to an integrated ritual of creation, drawing on the spiritual journey they have walked with Metatron. This phase focuses on advanced techniques that bring together all the teachings, aligning body, mind, and spirit in a final act of co-creation with the divine. With a profound sense of trust and a clear sense of purpose, the seeker prepares to manifest their intentions in alignment with the universal flow.

As the practice begins, Metatron invites the seeker to connect deeply with the energy of intention in the present moment. This practice, "Embracing the Now," centers on the idea that true manifestation does not exist in the distant future, nor in the expectations of what might be. Instead, the power of creation resides in the present, in the quiet and powerful focus of energy that emanates from the current moment. The seeker is encouraged to sit in meditation, feeling their intentions as if they are already real. Here, the mind is quieted, allowing the heart to become the primary channel, expressing a clear, loving vibration that invites the manifestation to become a living reality.

In the stillness of this presence, the seeker practices "Visualization of the Path," a technique that merges each step of the manifestation journey into a single, cohesive vision. Rather than focusing solely on the end goal, the seeker learns to visualize every stage of the journey, seeing the path as a continuous flow. By visualizing the steps toward their intentions, from small initial efforts to larger accomplishments, the seeker maintains clarity and devotion throughout the process. This path-oriented visualization fosters patience, as it invites the seeker to see each stage as a crucial element in the creation, trusting that each step unfolds in perfect timing.

As they deepen in this visualization, Metatron introduces "The Dance of the Elements." This practice aligns the seeker's intention with the four elements—earth, water, fire, and air—each one lending its energy to fortify and enrich the manifestation process. In meditation, the seeker feels the grounding strength of earth, solidifying their resolve and giving structure to their dreams. Water brings fluidity, helping the seeker release resistance and adapt to changes. Fire ignites passion and clarity, empowering the will to manifest with courage, while air lends inspiration, lifting the intention to a higher plane where it aligns with divine wisdom. With each element's guidance, the seeker discovers a balanced approach to manifestation, honoring the need for grounded action, emotional harmony, inner passion, and mental clarity.

Metatron then leads the seeker into the "Ritual of Sacred Creation." This is a formal ceremony in which the seeker gathers symbolic elements that represent their intention, creating an altar space where these items hold energy and purpose. In this sacred space, the seeker arranges crystals, candles, and sacred objects, each one resonating with an aspect of their intention. Metatron's presence guides this ritual, encouraging the seeker to charge each item with their focused energy, visualizing the altar as a microcosm of their larger vision. As they sit before the altar, they silently affirm their intentions, asking for divine support and blessing. This sacred space becomes a reminder of the manifestation process, a focal point of concentrated energy that continues to resonate even after the ritual is complete.

Within this ceremony, Metatron introduces "The Offering of Surrender." In this part of the ritual, the seeker acknowledges the limit of their personal will, understanding that true manifestation flows from a partnership with the universe. The seeker takes a symbolic object, something precious to them, and offers it as a representation of surrender. This act is not one of loss but of profound release, allowing the seeker to let go of control, placing their trust in the divine. Through this offering, the seeker signals their willingness to allow their intention to be shaped, expanded, or transformed in alignment with their highest good.

Following the ritual, the seeker moves into "The Meditation of Gratitude," a practice that focuses on expressing thanks for both what has been manifested and what is yet to come. This gratitude is expansive, recognizing not only the blessings in the physical world but also the spiritual growth that has taken place throughout the journey. Metatron teaches that gratitude is a powerful force that elevates energy, making it easier for the universe to respond in kind. By filling the heart with gratitude, the seeker amplifies their alignment with abundance, shifting from a state of longing to a state of fulfillment.

At this point, Metatron guides the seeker through "The Mirror of Reflection," a final introspective exercise in which the seeker examines the process they have undergone. In this exercise, they reflect on their growth, observing how each challenge has strengthened their character and brought clarity to their intentions. Through the mirror of reflection, the seeker gains a new perspective on their journey, appreciating the ways in which each lesson has prepared them to manifest with wisdom and love. This reflection solidifies the seeker's understanding that manifestation is as much an internal process as an external one, rooted in self-discovery and personal transformation.

The section concludes with "The Prayer of Alignment," a prayer that invites the seeker to speak directly to the divine, expressing their desires and surrendering them to the flow of life. With Metatron's presence, the seeker offers their intentions as an act of love, asking for guidance, wisdom, and courage to walk their path with integrity. The prayer becomes an affirmation of trust, echoing the universal truth that every intention, when offered with an open heart, has the potential to manifest in ways beyond imagination.

Chapter 22
Spiritual Self-Care

Spiritual self-care emerges as a deep, inward journey, rooted in understanding the power of maintaining balance and nurturing one's spirit. In this phase, the focus turns to developing practices that nourish the connection with oneself, restoring peace, and revitalizing the inner energy fields. With Archangel Metatron's guidance, these self-care rituals are imbued with intention, serving as pillars for spiritual health and an alignment with divine purpose.

At the heart of self-care lies the simple act of daily presence and mindfulness. The seeker is encouraged to start each day with a "Morning Ritual of Awareness," a gentle exercise in which they greet the dawn not as an ordinary moment but as a sacred one. This ritual involves a few minutes of conscious breathing, grounding in the energy of a new day, and calling upon Metatron's light to envelop their energy field. With each breath, they visualize Metatron's radiance filling every cell, protecting and uplifting, awakening a sense of gratitude for life and its possibilities. By establishing this practice, the seeker cultivates resilience, entering each day with clarity and a heart-centered focus.

Following this, Metatron introduces "The Sacred Pause." This practice serves as a reminder to rest and reconnect with one's spirit throughout the day. The Sacred Pause invites the seeker to momentarily withdraw from the busyness of life, even if just for a few breaths, to center their awareness. By closing their eyes and taking three deep breaths, they can reconnect with

Metatron's presence, feeling the protective shield around them, gaining renewed clarity and strength. This act, though simple, is transformative; it anchors the seeker, offering a moment of sanctuary in the midst of daily demands.

Metatron then shares "The Evening Ritual of Release." This practice is a pathway to releasing accumulated energies from the day. In this ritual, the seeker visualizes any tension, worry, or negativity collected during the day leaving their body with each exhale. As they breathe deeply, they let go of stress, visualizing it dissipating like dark mist. They then imagine Metatron's light filling the void, bringing calm, protection, and a sense of purity. This daily release is a powerful way to cleanse the energy field, ensuring that the mind and body are unburdened as the seeker moves into rest. This practice becomes a bridge between the day's activities and the rejuvenation of sleep, paving the way for deeper, restorative rest.

In addition to these daily practices, Metatron introduces the seeker to "The Ritual of Bathing in Light." Here, the seeker uses water as a conduit for spiritual cleansing and restoration. In this ritual, they visualize the water imbued with Metatron's light, transforming it into a healing element. As the water flows over them, it carries away physical and energetic impurities, refreshing the body and spirit. This act of intentional cleansing not only purifies but also revitalizes, allowing the seeker to experience each bath as a rebirth of sorts, reconnecting them to their spiritual vitality.

Central to spiritual self-care is the concept of "Nourishing the Sacred Vessel," emphasizing that the physical body is the vessel through which spiritual work is carried out. The seeker is encouraged to treat their body with respect and awareness, acknowledging it as an essential partner on the spiritual path. They are guided to consume foods that bring vitality, avoiding those that deplete energy, and to engage in movement that honors the body's natural rhythms. Each meal becomes an opportunity for mindfulness, a practice of gratitude and acknowledgment for the nourishment received, reinforcing the understanding that physical care is inseparable from spiritual care.

Metatron further introduces the seeker to "The Power of the Personal Sanctuary." This space, no matter how simple, is a dedicated corner or altar within the home. It serves as a personal sanctuary where the seeker can retreat to reconnect with their essence and with Metatron's energy. Adorned with elements that resonate—perhaps a candle, a crystal, or sacred symbols—this space becomes a focal point for grounding practices, meditation, and renewal. The personal sanctuary is a physical representation of the inner space that the seeker cultivates within; a place that invites quiet reflection and sacred stillness.

In nurturing their self-care, the seeker is also invited to practice "Mindful Silence." Once a week, they commit to a short period of silence, disconnecting from external distractions and immersing themselves in the tranquility that silence provides. In these moments, they simply observe, listening to the subtle whispers of their spirit, noticing thoughts as they arise without judgment, and allowing space for insights to surface. Through silence, they create a channel for inner clarity, attuning more deeply to their inner voice and the gentle presence of Metatron. This silence is not an absence but a presence, rich with potential for healing and insight.

Another essential self-care practice introduced by Metatron is "The Invocation of Personal Boundaries." This ritual calls for visualizing a protective sphere around the body, an energetic boundary infused with Metatron's light, shielding the seeker from negativity. This sphere is both porous and protective, allowing love and positivity to flow through, while filtering out harmful or draining energies. The seeker reinforces this boundary each morning with an invocation, affirming their right to maintain a space that honors their well-being. This boundary is not merely defensive; it becomes a testament to the seeker's commitment to self-respect and energetic health.

To close this first part on spiritual self-care, Metatron offers "The Prayer of Gentle Renewal," a prayer for restoring energy, bringing comfort, and fostering resilience. Each evening, the seeker expresses gratitude for the lessons of the day, offering any burdens to the divine and inviting Metatron's presence to fill their heart. This prayer, spoken softly or silently, serves as a nightly balm, allowing the seeker to surrender worries and find peace. Through these acts of care, the seeker transforms their daily routines into sacred rituals, building a foundation of spiritual wellness that supports and strengthens the ongoing journey.

The journey of spiritual self-care deepens into a more refined set of practices, focusing on personal empowerment and a strong alignment with Metatron's guidance. This section introduces methods for maintaining energetic stability, cultivating inner peace, and further enriching the relationship between self-care and spiritual growth. With each practice, the seeker is led to create a routine that is both meaningful and transformative, allowing self-care to become a cornerstone of their spiritual path.

Metatron begins by presenting the seeker with "The Breath of Alignment," a breathing technique designed to anchor the mind and elevate the spirit. In this practice, the seeker inhales deeply, visualizing Metatron's light filling their lungs and spreading throughout the body. As they exhale, they release tension and doubt, creating space for clarity and resilience. This breathwork is a reminder of the sacred connection between breath and life force, a tool for immediate grounding in moments of stress or fatigue. The Breath of Alignment can be practiced daily, especially before entering situations that require centeredness and composure, serving as a quiet invocation of Metatron's presence.

To amplify the effectiveness of their self-care, Metatron introduces "The Ritual of Energetic Shielding." This practice strengthens the seeker's protective aura, surrounding them in a sphere of light that both guards and uplifts. In this ritual, the seeker visualizes a radiant shield forming around their body, illuminated with Metatron's energy. This shield is not only protective; it is also a vessel for inner calm and clarity, allowing the seeker to navigate the world with a steady sense of security. By setting this energetic boundary each morning, the seeker reinforces their intent to maintain a balanced and protected energy field, which is especially valuable when facing stressful environments or emotionally intense interactions.

A critical aspect of self-care is fostering resilience, which Metatron addresses through "The Mantra of Inner Strength." This mantra is a simple but powerful affirmation that the seeker can repeat silently or aloud: "I am anchored in the light; I am protected, I am at peace." This affirmation aligns the mind with a state of inner fortitude, inviting peace into the body and spirit. The Mantra of Inner Strength serves as a personal touchstone, a reminder of the seeker's capability to remain balanced and composed, regardless of external challenges. By using this mantra consistently, the seeker gradually builds an internal foundation of unwavering resilience, harmonizing with Metatron's steady support.

Further enriching the self-care practice, Metatron introduces "The Crystal of Connection," a ritual involving the intentional use of crystals to enhance and stabilize energy. The seeker selects a crystal that resonates with their current intentions—amethyst for clarity, rose quartz for love, or black tourmaline for grounding. By holding the crystal and setting an intention, the seeker forms a tangible link to the Earth's energy, inviting the crystal to act as both a spiritual ally and a tool for empowerment. This practice, combined with regular cleansing of the crystal, ensures that the seeker's environment is one of continuous positive energy, reinforcing their connection to Metatron and universal forces.

In addition to crystal work, Metatron encourages the "Herbal Bath of Renewal." This ritual uses specific herbs such as lavender, rosemary, or chamomile, steeped in hot water to create a calming, rejuvenating bath. The seeker visualizes Metatron's light infusing the water, transforming it into a pool of healing energy. As they bathe, they release mental and emotional burdens, allowing the water to cleanse their spirit and restore vitality. This practice serves as an act of both physical and spiritual renewal, a way to wash away negativity and return to a place of peace and balance.

As the seeker builds these rituals, they are encouraged to weave in "The Practice of Silent Listening." In moments of stillness, the seeker listens not only to the external world but to the subtle currents of intuition and divine guidance within. In the silence, Metatron's presence becomes more perceptible, as insights and messages emerge from within the depths of the seeker's own consciousness. This practice deepens the seeker's relationship with their intuition, helping them recognize Metatron's influence as a quiet, guiding force that supports their self-care and spiritual alignment.

To sustain these practices, Metatron introduces "The Circle of Gratitude." This ritual invites the seeker to close each day with a short reflection on moments of gratitude, honoring both small and profound blessings. In a journal or through mental reflection, the seeker lists three things they are grateful for, releasing any attachments or concerns as they prepare for rest. By focusing on gratitude, the seeker elevates their vibrational frequency, fostering a state of openness and joy. The Circle of Gratitude reinforces an attitude of appreciation, which, over time, attracts more positive experiences and strengthens the seeker's connection with Metatron's benevolent energy.

Lastly, Metatron introduces "The Daily Seal of Light," a final evening ritual that closes each day with an invocation of protection and peace. Before sleep, the seeker envisions a soft, glowing light encasing their body, filling their mind and heart with tranquility. In this sacred space, they invite Metatron's guidance to guard their dreams and grant them restorative rest. This practice brings closure to the day's events, allowing the seeker to surrender fully into relaxation, trusting that their energy is shielded and supported through the night.

By embracing these self-care practices, the seeker builds a sanctuary within, anchored in daily acts of respect for body, mind, and spirit. Each ritual becomes a means of harmonizing with Metatron's light, deepening the seeker's connection to their own essence, and fostering an environment of enduring peace and stability. This commitment to self-care transcends the individual, creating ripples of harmony that uplift and inspire all aspects of life.

Chapter 23
Gratitude and Abundance

The energy of gratitude opens a powerful channel to abundance, harmonizing the spirit with the flow of universal blessings. In the first journey into this theme, the focus turns to cultivating a state of gratitude, an internal practice that shifts perception and invites deeper connections with life's gifts. With Metatron as the guiding presence, the seeker learns how a spirit anchored in appreciation not only transforms one's mindset but also draws forth abundance in both spiritual and material forms.

Metatron begins with the "Awakening of Gratitude," a daily practice of mindful reflection. The seeker is invited to set aside a few moments each morning to recognize three aspects of life for which they feel grateful. These can range from the beauty of nature to acts of kindness or a moment of clarity. As the seeker acknowledges these blessings, Metatron's presence becomes a supportive force, amplifying their sense of appreciation and grounding them in the present moment. This awakening creates an inner warmth that fills the day with intention, establishing gratitude as the foundation for all actions and interactions.

An essential aspect of practicing gratitude lies in recognizing both visible and hidden blessings. Metatron introduces the "Blessings Unseen" meditation, a contemplative journey where the seeker reflects on challenges that, upon deeper reflection, have served a purpose in their growth. Through this meditation, the seeker learns to identify how past obstacles became catalysts for transformation, reshaping their path. By embracing these experiences as gifts, the seeker learns to perceive life's dualities with a more open heart, dissolving resistance and allowing gratitude to illuminate even the most difficult experiences. With each practice, gratitude becomes less conditional, expanding to embrace the full spectrum of life.

As the seeker strengthens their gratitude, Metatron encourages the use of "Gratitude Anchors" throughout the day. These are simple reminders—a small stone, a bracelet, or a favorite piece of nature—that the seeker can carry as symbols of appreciation. Each time the seeker notices their chosen anchor, they are prompted to pause, breathe, and acknowledge something meaningful in that moment. These anchors serve as a physical touchpoint, helping the seeker bring their awareness back to gratitude whenever they feel stressed or distracted. Over time, these moments accumulate, weaving gratitude into the fabric of daily life and increasing the seeker's vibrational frequency.

Metatron then presents the practice of "The Written Invocation," encouraging the seeker to keep a gratitude journal. In this journal, they record experiences and people they are thankful for, describing each with detail and heartfelt acknowledgment. Writing down these reflections strengthens their resonance, turning gratitude into a deeply rooted part of the seeker's consciousness. By revisiting these entries, the seeker creates a repository of positive energy, a source of comfort and perspective during challenging times. This written practice serves as an intimate ritual of reflection, where each word and memory becomes a step towards a more abundant mindset.

In the pursuit of abundance, Metatron introduces the seeker to the concept of "Appreciative Visualization." Here, the seeker learns to focus on desires from a place of gratitude rather than lack. With Metatron's guidance, they visualize their goals as already fulfilled, creating mental imagery of their life enriched by the realization of these dreams. By seeing their aspirations through the lens of gratitude, they shift their energy, aligning with the natural flow of the universe. This visualization invites abundance as an extension of appreciation, rather than as something distant or out of reach, turning dreams into seeds ready to flourish in the soil of genuine thankfulness.

An advanced practice, the "Gratitude Mandala," is then introduced as a form of creative expression. In this ritual, the seeker gathers objects from nature—stones, leaves, or flowers—to create a circular arrangement symbolizing unity and interconnectedness. As they place each item, they silently acknowledge a specific blessing in their life. When completed, this mandala becomes a tangible representation of gratitude, embodying the energy of abundance in a visual, sacred form. The mandala can remain in place as a living altar, radiating positive energy into the space, or be returned to nature in an act of offering, reinforcing the cycle of giving and receiving.

Metatron then presents "The Ripple of Giving," a practice that extends gratitude into the community. Here, the seeker is encouraged to perform acts of kindness, large or small, as expressions of appreciation for the abundance they experience. Whether by offering time, resources, or words of encouragement, these gestures allow the seeker to share their gratitude in tangible ways. Through this ripple effect, gratitude transforms into a source of light, connecting the seeker with others and reinforcing their alignment with the universe's flow of giving and receiving.

Metatron introduces "The Nightly Gratitude Reflection," a brief evening practice of revisiting the day's moments of gratitude. As the seeker prepares for rest, they mentally review any blessings or moments of grace they encountered. By closing the day with this reflection, the seeker invites peace into their heart, allowing gratitude to shape both their waking and resting states. This ritual sets a tone of calm and fulfillment for the night, ensuring that they enter sleep with a mind attuned to abundance and harmony.

With these practices, the seeker's understanding of gratitude evolves from a fleeting feeling to an enduring state of being. As gratitude becomes an integral part of daily life, it opens channels to abundance that transcend material wealth, fostering a deep, inner richness that aligns with Metatron's guiding light.

Through these layers of appreciation, the seeker is empowered to embrace life with an open heart, cultivating a path illuminated by the energy of boundless gratitude and prosperity.

As gratitude deepens, it becomes a magnetic force, drawing abundance into every aspect of life. In this continued exploration, Metatron guides the seeker through refined practices designed to enhance the vibrational frequency of gratitude, encouraging not only the attraction of material blessings but the expansion of spiritual richness. Through these methods, gratitude becomes a powerful means of alignment, tuning the seeker to the harmonious frequencies of universal energy.

One of the first techniques Metatron introduces is "Affirmative Expression," a practice that uses spoken words to resonate with higher vibrations. The seeker is encouraged to begin each day by vocalizing affirmations that express their gratitude and desires. Examples include statements like, "I am grateful for the abundance that flows into my life" or "I am aligned with the frequency of gratitude and prosperity." These affirmations, spoken with intention, become powerful declarations that shift the mind and spirit towards receiving. As the seeker repeats these statements daily, they begin to shape their reality, inviting the energy of abundance into their thoughts, actions, and surroundings.

The power of Metatron's guidance is further deepened in "Gratitude Breathwork," a technique that combines mindful breathing with focused appreciation. Here, the seeker is instructed to inhale deeply, drawing in the energy of gratitude, and exhale with an intentional release of any thoughts of lack or limitation. As they continue this cycle of breath, Metatron's presence serves as a gentle force of purification, aiding the seeker in expanding their heart with each breath. This practice can be performed whenever feelings of scarcity arise, acting as a cleansing ritual that clears the mind and reinforces a state of receptivity to abundance.

To elevate the connection with Metatron, the seeker is introduced to "The Sacred Altar of Gratitude." This altar, built with symbols of personal blessings, becomes a focal point for daily gratitude rituals. Metatron suggests including objects that resonate with abundance, such as candles, crystals, and representations of nature's beauty. Each item is placed with a specific intention, acknowledging a particular aspect of life for which the seeker is grateful. This altar is not only a visual reminder of abundance but a spiritual space where the seeker can connect deeply with gratitude, engaging in daily moments of reflection and appreciation in a sacred setting. Over time, the altar becomes a magnet for positive energy, amplifying the flow of blessings into the seeker's life.

To amplify the reach of gratitude, Metatron introduces "The Gratitude Ripple Practice," an exercise in expressing thanks beyond the self. In this practice, the seeker reaches out to others with words of appreciation. Whether through a message, a handwritten note, or a spoken acknowledgment, this act of expressing gratitude becomes a living exchange of energy. By sharing appreciation with those around them, the seeker participates in the creation of a network of abundance, where each grateful thought contributes to the greater flow of positive energy. This practice transforms gratitude from a personal experience into a shared resonance, building an environment that nurtures both the self and others.

Metatron's teachings then guide the seeker to "The Gratitude Walk," a meditative journey in nature where each step is taken with mindful appreciation. During this walk, the seeker is encouraged to observe their surroundings—the warmth of sunlight, the strength of trees, the softness of earth beneath their feet. As they move through this natural space, they silently offer thanks for each element they encounter. This practice becomes a grounding ritual, reminding the seeker of their interconnectedness with the world around them and inviting them to absorb nature's abundance into their being. The Gratitude Walk instills a profound sense of peace, aligning the seeker with the rhythm of life itself.

The connection to gratitude and abundance reaches further depth in "The Visualization of Future Abundance." Here, Metatron guides the seeker to visualize a future filled with fulfillment, peace, and joy. In this visualization, the seeker envisions their life as if all desires have already manifested—seeing themselves surrounded by supportive relationships, fulfilling work, and a sense of purpose. As they hold this vision, Metatron helps them feel the gratitude for this reality as though it already exists. This practice not only clarifies the seeker's goals but plants the seeds of abundance within their spirit, aligning them with the potential of future blessings that are already present within their energy field.

Metatron then introduces "The Ritual of Water Offering," a symbolic act of gratitude and letting go. In this ritual, the seeker pours a small amount of water into a natural body of water, such as a river, lake, or even a personal altar bowl, while silently expressing thanks for the blessings they have received. This offering acknowledges the cycles of giving and receiving, reinforcing the understanding that gratitude is a flowing energy, not a static one. The water ritual reminds the seeker of the impermanence of life's moments and the importance of appreciating each experience fully. This simple, profound act becomes a ritual of humility and a reminder of the interconnectedness of all things.

The section concludes with "The Circle of Abundance," a powerful gathering where the seeker invites close friends or family members to share in a collective ritual of gratitude. This circle, blessed by Metatron's energy, is formed with each participant taking turns to express what they are grateful for, fostering a communal atmosphere of appreciation. Through this collective energy, gratitude is magnified, and the circle becomes a space where each individual contributes to the abundant energy shared among all. This gathering not only strengthens bonds but reinforces the lesson that gratitude, when shared, multiplies in strength and effect.

With these advanced practices, gratitude becomes more than an individual experience; it becomes a transformative energy that reshapes the seeker's relationship with the universe. As Metatron's guidance unfolds, the seeker learns that abundance is not an external state to be attained but an internal energy to be cultivated and shared. The path of gratitude opens doorways to profound abundance, enriching the seeker's spirit and inviting the universe to respond in kind. Through these practices, gratitude ceases to be a reaction to blessings and instead becomes the creative force behind them, allowing the seeker to embrace each moment as part of an endless flow of universal blessings.

Chapter 24
Aura Strengthening

The aura, a luminous field surrounding every being, serves as both a reflection and protector of one's inner state. In Metatron's teachings, the aura is not merely an energy shield but a dynamic extension of the soul, constantly interacting with the vibrations around it. Strengthening this vital field is essential to achieving spiritual clarity, emotional resilience, and alignment with higher frequencies.

In his guidance, Metatron introduces "The Light Expansion Technique," a fundamental practice designed to empower the aura's protective qualities. Here, the seeker visualizes a golden light beginning at the center of their heart, radiating outward to create a sphere that encircles the entire body. With each breath, this light becomes brighter, more radiant, reinforcing the aura's resilience. This expanding energy fills any weak points in the aura, creating an impenetrable layer of light that wards off negativity and promotes a sense of security and inner peace. The Light Expansion Technique becomes a daily ritual, grounding the seeker in the strength of their own energy and fortifying their boundaries against external influences.

Next, Metatron introduces the seeker to "Aura Cleansing with Crystals," a method for removing stagnant or unwanted energy from the aura. The seeker is encouraged to use cleansing crystals like selenite, amethyst, or black tourmaline, holding them in one hand and moving them in gentle circles around the body. Metatron's guidance emphasizes intentionality: as the seeker moves the crystal, they focus on releasing all residual energies that no longer serve them, replacing these with clarity and positivity. This practice is particularly effective after challenging encounters or at the end of a long day, allowing the seeker to shed accumulated energies and restore their natural frequency.

In Metatron's teachings, grounding is also essential to strengthening the aura. He introduces the "Rooted Aura Technique," which connects the aura to the stabilizing energy of the Earth. This practice begins with the seeker visualizing roots growing from the soles of their feet deep into the Earth's core, grounding them firmly. Through these roots, Earth energy flows upward, filling the aura with a dense, protective energy. This connection to Earth not only strengthens the aura's resilience but also harmonizes it with nature, adding a layer of grounded stability to the seeker's spiritual defenses.

Metatron then teaches the seeker "Aura Breathing," a technique that harmonizes breathing with aura expansion. In this practice, the seeker inhales deeply, imagining that they are breathing in universal energy, and exhales while visualizing that energy radiating out from their body into their aura. Each exhale expands the aura, reinforcing its strength and density. This method is particularly powerful when performed outdoors or near natural elements, where the surrounding energy can assist in building a resilient and harmonious aura. Aura Breathing becomes a way of not only strengthening but also nurturing the aura, helping it resonate at a frequency that attracts positive experiences and repels negativity.

Another key technique is "Aura Sealing with Essential Oils." Metatron recommends oils known for their protective and purifying properties, such as lavender, frankincense, or sandalwood. The seeker applies a small amount of oil to their wrists, temples, or heart center, and, through intention, infuses their aura with the energy of the oil's scent and vibration. Each essential oil is chosen for a specific quality—lavender for peace, frankincense for purification, sandalwood for grounding. As the aroma permeates the air, the aura absorbs these qualities, enhancing its protective capabilities and uplifting the seeker's energy.

Metatron's teachings also emphasize the importance of aura attunement with natural elements, especially the purifying power of sunlight and moonlight. In the "Solar and Lunar Aura Bath" practice, the seeker exposes themselves to the gentle warmth of the morning sun or the calm energy of the moon, allowing their aura to absorb these natural frequencies. The sun's energy invigorates, filling the aura with vitality, while the moon's energy cleanses and soothes, easing any inner turbulence. By regularly connecting with these celestial energies, the seeker finds a renewed balance within their aura, aligning it with both the cycles of nature and the flow of cosmic rhythms.

Metatron introduces the seeker to "Sacred Sound Cleansing," using sound as a tool for aura strengthening. Instruments such as bells, singing bowls, or tuning forks emit frequencies that resonate with the aura, dissolving energetic blockages and filling the field with harmonious vibrations. The seeker chooses a sound instrument and moves it slowly around their body, allowing the sound to permeate their aura. Each note resonates through the layers of the aura, lifting away any stagnant energy and replacing it with clarity and tranquility. Sacred Sound Cleansing becomes a ritual that can be used whenever the aura feels heavy or clouded, clearing the energetic field and restoring it to its natural state.

As the seeker progresses, Metatron introduces the concept of "Aura Shielding through Visualization." This technique invites the seeker to envision a crystalline barrier around their aura, a protective yet transparent shield that allows only positive energy to pass through. Metatron suggests a color for this shield based on the seeker's needs: a blue light for calm, a green light for healing, or a violet light for spiritual protection. This shield is not static; rather, it is a living energy that adapts to the seeker's needs, serving as a layer of protection against negative influences and unwanted energies.

Metatron guides the seeker through "The Ritual of Aura Blessing," a practice where they affirm their gratitude and respect for the aura's role in protecting and guiding them. The seeker places one hand over their heart and the other at their solar plexus, sending love and appreciation to their aura. They affirm, "I honor and strengthen my aura, the field that reflects and protects my true essence." This blessing ritual becomes a way to actively acknowledge and reinforce the aura's importance, creating a bond of care and mutual respect between the seeker and their energy field.

As these practices unfold, the seeker learns that aura strengthening is more than an exercise in protection—it is an act of nurturing, an honoring of one's own energetic boundaries and spiritual space. With Metatron's guidance, each layer of the aura becomes fortified, each energy point aligned with the protective forces of the universe. This is not just a series of techniques but an invitation to embrace the aura as a living shield, a luminous field that reflects the seeker's journey toward spiritual mastery. Through these teachings, the seeker becomes not only protected but empowered, standing with confidence within their own radiant energy.

Building on the initial practices of aura strengthening, Metatron's teachings now guide the seeker into deeper, more transformative rituals that expand and fortify their energy field. The practices here are designed not only to protect but also to amplify the aura, creating a radiant, high-frequency field that attracts harmony and repels negativity. These techniques engage the power of visualization, ritual, and natural energies to create a lasting connection between the aura and the divine realms.

Metatron introduces the seeker to "The Mirror of Light" technique, where they visualize their aura as a mirror reflecting only positive energies. In this practice, the seeker imagines a radiant mirror surrounding their aura, which not only shields them but also amplifies beneficial energies. As they focus on this mirror, they perceive it reflecting divine light back into the world, creating a continuous exchange of positivity. This technique transforms the aura into an active participant in spreading light, making the aura a conduit for uplifting vibrations.

Another advanced practice, "The Elemental Aura Infusion," involves calling upon the four elements—Earth, Water, Fire, and Air—to reinforce and balance the aura. Under Metatron's guidance, the seeker visualizes each element energizing a quadrant of their aura. The Earth element, symbolized as a green light, brings stability; Water, as a flowing blue energy, offers emotional healing; Fire, with its vibrant orange or red hue, ignites strength and courage; and Air, represented by a soft white or silver glow, enhances clarity and wisdom. This ritual of infusion aligns the aura with the universal forces, creating a harmonious and resilient energy field.

Metatron then introduces "Aura Anchoring with Sacred Geometry." In this visualization, the seeker calls upon symbols such as Metatron's Cube to strengthen the aura's structure. The seeker envisions this sacred geometry forming within and around the aura, creating a matrix of protection and strength. Each line and intersection in the cube connects with the seeker's energy centers, amplifying the aura's stability and resonance with divine frequencies. This sacred geometry functions as both a shield and a guide, aligning the aura with universal patterns and fostering an innate sense of order and purpose.

In his wisdom, Metatron shares "The Golden Veil of Peace" meditation, a practice that infuses the aura with a calming, restorative energy. The seeker visualizes a gentle, golden veil descending around their aura, enveloping them in a warm, protective embrace. This veil softens harsh energies and brings a deep sense of peace, which the seeker absorbs with each breath. The Golden Veil becomes a comforting layer of protection, one that diffuses external stress and nurtures a serene inner state. This technique is especially helpful during times of emotional turbulence, creating a sanctuary within the aura.

For enhanced protection, Metatron teaches "Aura Sealing with Ritual Smoke," using sacred herbs such as sage, palo santo, or lavender. The seeker burns these herbs and allows the smoke to surround their aura, purifying and sealing it from any disruptive energies. This smoke acts as both a cleanser and a sealant, solidifying the aura's boundary. As the smoke dissipates, the seeker visualizes their aura shining more brightly, free from any lingering energies that do not align with their highest purpose. This practice creates a sanctified space around the seeker, a protected and energetically purified zone that remains unbroken.

To elevate the aura's vibration further, Metatron introduces "Vocal Harmonization," a technique using sound as a way to stabilize and elevate the aura. The seeker chants specific tones, such as "OM" or "AH," which resonate with the chakras and amplify the aura's strength. These sounds create vibrational waves that move through the energy field, dispersing any dense or stagnant energy. The practice of Vocal Harmonization not only strengthens the aura but also aligns it with higher frequencies, connecting the seeker's energy field with the harmonious vibrations of the universe.

In the next phase, Metatron guides the seeker through "The Aura Expansion Visualization," a technique that allows the seeker to feel their aura stretching beyond its immediate boundary, reaching out to connect with universal energy. The seeker visualizes their aura expanding in concentric waves, first encompassing the room, then the building, and finally merging with the light of the cosmos. This expansion not only strengthens the aura's resilience but also allows the seeker to feel part of a greater spiritual tapestry. Through this technique, the aura becomes vast, inclusive, and resonant with the interconnectedness of all things.

Another transformative practice Metatron offers is "Aura Illumination through Breathwork." In this technique, the seeker performs focused breathing exercises, breathing in light with each inhale and expanding their aura with each exhale. This breathwork charges the aura with light, making it bright and impenetrable. With each breath, the aura becomes more luminous, radiating a protective, high-frequency glow that attracts only beneficial energies. The steady rhythm of breathwork aligns the seeker with the essence of life, allowing them to reinforce their aura with every breath.

To harmonize the emotional layers of the aura, Metatron introduces "Heart-Centered Aura Healing." This practice invites the seeker to focus on their heart chakra, imagining a radiant pink or green light emanating from this center and filling the aura. This heart-centered energy brings warmth, compassion, and resilience, creating an aura that is not only strong but also open to love and understanding. Heart-Centered Aura Healing is particularly useful in times of relational challenges, as it strengthens the aura's emotional resilience and helps the seeker maintain a balanced, compassionate outlook.

As a final, comprehensive practice, Metatron guides the seeker through "The Crystal Light Grid," a ritual where specific crystals are arranged in a sacred geometric pattern around the seeker to enhance the aura's protection and alignment. Crystals such as clear quartz, amethyst, and rose quartz are placed in a circle, forming a grid that radiates harmonious energy. The seeker sits at the center of this grid, feeling the energy of the crystals infusing their aura, sealing and reinforcing it with pure light. This grid not only fortifies the aura but also attunes it to the healing frequencies of the crystal kingdom, establishing a deep connection to Earth's natural energies.

Each of these techniques deepens the connection between the seeker and their aura, empowering them to maintain an energy field that is both resilient and receptive. As the seeker continues to practice these advanced methods, the aura becomes a beacon of light, a radiant shield that honors and reflects the journey within. Metatron's teachings reveal that a strengthened aura is not merely a shield against the world but a bridge to it—an invitation to engage with life from a place of wholeness, clarity, and alignment with the highest frequencies of love and light. Through these practices, the seeker's aura transforms, embodying the balance, wisdom, and strength that Metatron imparts.

Chapter 25
Spiritual Service

In the unfolding journey with Archangel Metatron, spiritual service emerges as a fundamental path to elevate consciousness and deepen the connection with divine energy. Metatron reveals that true service is not merely about actions or deeds but a reflection of the soul's commitment to unity with all life. In serving others, the seeker connects to a higher purpose, fostering a sense of interconnectedness and love that transcends the self.

Metatron introduces the seeker to the ancient concept of "Service as Sacrament," where every act of compassion, kindness, or generosity becomes a sacred ritual. He guides the seeker to approach service with a heart centered on love, encouraging them to perceive each interaction as an opportunity to honor the divine spark within others. Through this lens, service transcends duty, transforming into an act of devotion that nourishes the soul and enriches the spirit of those served.

An essential aspect of spiritual service lies in the art of "Presence." Metatron explains that being fully present with others—whether in listening, assisting, or simply sharing a moment—carries a healing power of its own. By cultivating deep awareness in each encounter, the seeker learns to channel divine energy, offering more than words or actions alone could provide. Presence becomes a conduit for Metatron's light, allowing the seeker to bring peace and comfort to those they touch.

Metatron also emphasizes the importance of discernment in spiritual service, reminding the seeker to remain aligned with their own energy boundaries. True service respects both the giver and receiver, fostering an exchange that uplifts both without diminishing either. Metatron teaches that balance in service is vital, guiding the seeker in setting healthy limits to avoid burnout and maintain a steady flow of energy. This balance allows the seeker to serve sustainably, preserving their vitality for continued acts of love and support.

A key practice in spiritual service is "Silent Blessings." This subtle form of service involves offering blessings to others without seeking recognition. Whether passing by strangers, observing someone in need, or reflecting on loved ones, the seeker learns to send silent prayers of well-being, strength, and peace. These blessings ripple outward, influencing the energetic field of others, quietly supporting their journey. In this way, the seeker practices humility, nurturing a pure intention that seeks no reward, only the silent satisfaction of spreading light.

Metatron then introduces "The Ritual of Gratitude in Service," where the seeker consciously acknowledges the opportunity to serve. Before and after each act of service, they pause to give thanks, recognizing the sacredness of the exchange. By honoring the role they play in another's life, even momentarily, the seeker attunes to a sense of reverence. This ritual deepens their connection with the divine, transforming service from a simple act into a shared blessing.

To enhance the impact of their service, Metatron guides the seeker in "Energy Infusion for Acts of Service." Before engaging in any action intended to help or support others, the seeker visualizes filling their heart with divine light. They imagine this light expanding, flowing through their hands, voice, and presence. This energy infuses every action, allowing each act of service to carry a vibrational gift of love and healing. The seeker becomes a vessel of Metatron's light, amplifying the impact of their service on a spiritual level.

"Acts of Service as Meditation" is another profound approach Metatron teaches. By treating acts of service as a form of meditation, the seeker brings full attention and intentionality to each task, however small. In washing dishes, sweeping floors, or comforting a friend, the seeker maintains mindfulness, observing each motion, sound, and sensation. This practice transforms service into a living prayer, a moving meditation that centers the seeker in peace while benefiting others. Through this approach, service becomes a pathway to greater spiritual presence, heightening the seeker's connection to the divine.

Metatron also speaks of "Community and Collective Well-being," emphasizing the importance of extending service beyond the individual level to benefit communities. The seeker learns that by contributing to community efforts, sharing resources, or participating in group meditations, they engage in a broader network of light. This collective service strengthens bonds, unites diverse souls, and brings the divine closer to all involved. Through communal actions, the seeker witnesses the amplifying power of collective intention and feels the profound fulfillment of serving a greater cause.

"The Circle of Reflection" is introduced as a method to balance the inner and outer aspects of service. After engaging in acts of service, the seeker sets aside time to reflect on the experience. Metatron encourages them to ask reflective questions: What did I learn from this service? How did it open my heart? In what ways did it challenge me? By holding a mirror to their experiences, the seeker grows in self-awareness, discovering insights about their own spirit. This reflection strengthens their dedication to service, helping them align each action with deeper purpose and personal growth.

Lastly, Metatron introduces the concept of "Unity through Service." In each act of kindness or generosity, the seeker embraces a sense of oneness, recognizing that service to another is, in essence, service to oneself. Metatron explains that all beings are interconnected threads within the divine tapestry; as one thread is uplifted, so too is the entire fabric. Through this understanding, the seeker transcends separation, experiencing service as an expression of unity. This realization brings joy, as the seeker feels themselves woven into the universal flow of love, an integral part of something far greater than the self.

In exploring the practices and philosophies of spiritual service, the seeker begins to see service as a dynamic exchange of energies, a way to embody divine love actively. As Metatron guides them deeper into these practices, they recognize that spiritual service is more than an external duty—it is an inner commitment to live in harmony with the light within and around them. Each act of service becomes a stepping stone on the path of spiritual evolution, a way to deepen their alignment with Metatron's teachings, and a means to nurture the world through the sacred art of giving.

As the journey into spiritual service deepens, Metatron guides the seeker toward practices that cultivate an unwavering commitment to selfless service. Building upon the foundations of individual acts, Metatron now expands the vision, illuminating how sustained, conscious service can transform both the individual and the community. The seeker learns to embody a spiritual presence that uplifts all whom they encounter, channeling divine energy into the world.

One essential practice Metatron introduces is "Service as Divine Reflection." Through this lens, every act of kindness, from the smallest to the grandest, mirrors the divine. The seeker begins each day with a mindful intention to act as an instrument of Metatron's light, embracing humility and surrender. Through such a practice, they do not impose their will or desires but instead ask to serve in the way most aligned with the universe's needs. This daily dedication serves as a prayer in motion, connecting the seeker's actions to a higher source of guidance and wisdom.

"Deep Listening" becomes a foundational aspect of this service. Metatron teaches that true listening—one that reaches beyond words and gestures—opens a pathway for divine wisdom to flow. In listening deeply to others, the seeker silences their own thoughts and judgments, creating a space where they can connect to the essence of the other person. This act of profound listening becomes an invitation for the divine to enter the interaction, enabling the seeker to perceive unspoken needs and offer compassion that heals. Through deep listening, the seeker finds that they become more attuned to the spiritual currents within every exchange, transforming each encounter into a sacred connection.

Metatron then presents "Altruistic Energy Work," a practice that channels spiritual energy toward global healing and transformation. The seeker learns to focus their energy beyond immediate circles, directing it toward situations or regions in need, be it for environmental, social, or emotional healing. This energy work requires no physical proximity or recognition but rests in the quiet power of focused intention. Visualizing Metatron's light radiating outward, the seeker sends waves of peace and healing, contributing to a global tapestry of light. Over time, the seeker begins to see how their individual contributions, though seemingly small, are part of a vast web of compassion that interconnects the entire world.

To ensure sustainable engagement in service, Metatron underscores the significance of "Sacred Renewal Practices." The seeker is reminded that service, to remain effective, must come from a place of inner harmony and abundance. Regular self-care, meditation, and moments of quiet introspection become essential to replenishing the energy needed for continued service. Through these practices, the seeker honors the cycle of giving and receiving, recognizing that tending to one's own spirit is not selfish but rather foundational to effective and compassionate service.

In moments of service, Metatron encourages the seeker to practice "Spiritual Discernment." This discernment allows them to recognize when they are called to act and when it may be more beneficial to step back. Not every situation requires intervention; some challenges are growth opportunities for others. The seeker learns to tune into their inner guidance, discerning when their involvement is aligned with divine will. Metatron teaches that discernment nurtures a wise, mature approach to service, ensuring that each act arises from genuine intuition rather than a sense of obligation.

A profound aspect of service Metatron introduces is "Ritual of Sacred Offering." Before each act of service, the seeker engages in a short ritual, blessing their intention with a prayer or visualization. They may light a candle, recite a mantra, or silently call upon Metatron's guidance, imbuing the action with spiritual power. By consecrating their service, the seeker connects with the higher purpose behind each act, strengthening their alignment with divine energies and ensuring that their service flows from a pure and elevated source.

"Unity Circles" become a communal extension of the seeker's journey into spiritual service. Metatron guides the seeker to gather with others in shared practices of service, be it through group meditation, environmental efforts, or supporting vulnerable communities. Unity circles amplify the seeker's efforts, creating a powerful synergy as individuals join in a shared purpose. Together, they form a circle of light, combining energies in ways that elevate not only the individual members but also the collective consciousness. Through this experience, the seeker witnesses how group service multiplies their personal contributions, embodying the interconnectedness of all life.

Metatron introduces "Acts of Invisible Kindness," a practice of anonymous service that allows the seeker to engage in acts of love without expecting acknowledgment. These acts might be as simple as leaving a thoughtful note for a stranger, supporting a charitable cause, or contributing to community projects in silence. Invisible kindness invites the seeker to let go of personal recognition, reinforcing the purity of intention. Each unspoken gesture carries the quiet strength of true compassion, transforming the seeker as they experience the humility and joy of serving for the sake of service itself.

The journey into advanced service concludes with the transformative practice of "Gratitude in Reflection." At the end of each day, the seeker reflects on their acts of service, not as achievements, but as blessings they were privileged to share. By reviewing each moment with gratitude, the seeker reinforces their connection to Metatron's guidance, finding joy in both giving and receiving. This reflective gratitude deepens their humility and renews their commitment, strengthening the bridge between their spirit and the world they serve.

In this culmination of spiritual service, the seeker embraces a life of quiet devotion, humility, and boundless compassion. They become a living channel for Metatron's light, carrying peace, healing, and divine wisdom into each interaction, whether with a single individual or the collective world. Through these practices, the seeker transcends the illusion of separation, embodying the unity that connects all life, and fulfilling the sacred call to serve with an open and awakened heart.

Chapter 26
Connection with Ancestors

The journey into ancestral connection begins as a quiet invitation to discover the roots that nourish the soul. Metatron guides the seeker into a deeper exploration of their lineage, awakening a bridge between past and present, allowing the wisdom of ancestors to infuse spiritual growth and self-understanding. Through this connection, the seeker begins to see themselves not as an isolated being but as part of a vast lineage, a tapestry woven from the lives, choices, and experiences of those who came before.

One of the first practices Metatron introduces is the "Ritual of Ancestral Reverence." In this sacred practice, the seeker creates an altar or designated space honoring their lineage, whether it be through photos, symbols, or items that carry ancestral significance. This altar serves as a focal point for reflection and prayer, inviting the energies of the ancestors into the seeker's space. Here, the seeker lights a candle, focusing on each flicker as a gateway between worlds, opening a path for connection, remembrance, and gratitude. This altar becomes a living symbol of connection, a place to return to regularly for insight and communion with ancestral energy.

Metatron then introduces the seeker to the "Invocation of Ancestral Wisdom," a meditative practice that calls upon the insights and strength of those who have lived before. Sitting in stillness, the seeker visualizes themselves surrounded by a circle of ancestors, each one a bearer of wisdom and experience. In this meditation, the seeker allows questions or life challenges to arise in their heart, then opens their awareness, sensing guidance from the energies surrounding them. Through this act of invocation, the seeker begins to perceive subtle impressions, a flow of insights that may appear as thoughts, emotions, or images, often containing guidance shaped by the ancestral path.

In the practice of "Tracing the Bloodline," Metatron encourages the seeker to explore family history, stories, and connections. This act of inquiry is both a spiritual and personal journey, leading the seeker to discover qualities, talents, and values inherited through generations. The seeker is invited to document stories, perhaps by speaking to family members, reading letters, or recording memories. Each tale, each shared moment, is woven into the seeker's consciousness, allowing them to embrace the wisdom, struggles, and resilience held within their lineage. This practice brings forward a realization that their life is a continuation of a larger story, one where the choices of today become the legacy of tomorrow.

Metatron's guidance extends into the practice of "Healing Ancestral Patterns." Here, the seeker identifies recurring emotional, mental, or spiritual patterns that may have roots in ancestral trauma or unresolved energy. This practice involves working closely with the heart chakra, allowing compassion to flow toward any struggles, grief, or hardships experienced by ancestors. Through guided visualization, the seeker imagines sending healing light backward along the family line, breaking patterns that no longer serve and allowing peace to flow through generations. This transformative process not only aids the seeker in releasing limitations but also brings a sense of peace and release to the ancestral spirit.

Metatron encourages the seeker to engage in "Offerings of Gratitude," simple acts of remembrance to honor their ancestors. The seeker might leave flowers, light incense, or offer food in a symbolic gesture of respect. This offering is not merely ceremonial but a heart-centered expression of gratitude, a way of acknowledging the paths that were walked before, the sacrifices made, and the gifts passed down. Through these offerings, the seeker cultivates a bond with the unseen, deepening the sense of continuity and unity across time and space.

As the seeker develops this connection, Metatron reveals the importance of "Dream Work with Ancestors." In the quiet realm of dreams, ancestors often appear, offering insights or messages. Before sleep, the seeker may ask for guidance or understanding from their lineage, inviting dreams that bring clarity or healing. Keeping a journal by the bedside allows for recording these dream experiences, noting patterns, symbols, or feelings that may carry ancestral wisdom. Over time, this dream practice enhances the seeker's ability to discern and interpret the messages that arise, fostering a subtle yet profound connection to their roots.

In "Walking the Ancestral Path," the seeker learns to walk mindfully in places of significance to their family or cultural heritage. By visiting these locations—be they family homes, land, or places of heritage—the seeker connects physically with the spaces that held the lives and energy of their ancestors. Metatron encourages the seeker to walk with reverence, to breathe deeply, and to listen to the energy in these spaces, absorbing the memories and energies that linger. This physical act of connection grounds the seeker, strengthening the ties between their present path and the ancestral past.

Metatron then brings attention to the "Cycle of Forgiveness and Release," a transformative practice for healing any unresolved feelings toward ancestral actions or experiences. The seeker acknowledges that within every lineage, there may be experiences of pain, hardship, or conflict. In a state of meditative compassion, the seeker extends forgiveness toward any known or unknown wounds within their lineage, visualizing Metatron's light enveloping the entire ancestral line in a healing embrace. This practice releases bonds of resentment or sorrow, clearing energy pathways and allowing future generations to inherit an unburdened spiritual lineage.

To deepen the connection, Metatron guides the seeker in the "Prayer of Ancestral Blessing." In this quiet prayer, the seeker calls upon the positive qualities, strengths, and virtues of their ancestors, inviting these energies to flow into their own life. With each breath, the seeker feels these qualities—resilience, love, courage, or creativity—integrate into their being, infusing their path with ancestral blessings. This prayer becomes a bridge, inviting the best of the past to nurture the present, empowering the seeker to move forward with a strong, grounded spirit.

Through these practices, the seeker's understanding of identity shifts, evolving from a perception of individuality to a profound awareness of continuity and interdependence. By connecting with their ancestors, the seeker draws wisdom, strength, and purpose from a lineage that pulses with life, learning to walk with both the honor and responsibility of those who came before.

As the journey with ancestral connection deepens, the seeker finds themselves enveloped in a realm where the energies of their lineage intertwine with their own path. With Metatron as a guide, the seeker embarks on practices designed to strengthen this bond, inviting the presence of ancestors into daily life and spiritual practice.

One profound method Metatron introduces is the "Ritual of Ancestral Invocation," a sacred ceremony where the seeker opens a channel to directly communicate with ancestors. In a quiet space, the seeker begins by lighting a candle, symbolizing the eternal flame of ancestral wisdom. Through focused breathing, they enter a meditative state, envisioning a circle of ancestors surrounding them. This ritual serves as a conduit, a place where the seeker can ask questions, seek guidance, and listen with an open heart, receiving messages from generations past. Metatron's light surrounds this gathering, acting as a protective energy that ensures the messages are received with clarity and peace.

Another practice, "The Path of Ancestral Dreams," encourages the seeker to strengthen their connection with ancestors through intentional dreamwork. Guided by Metatron, the seeker engages in pre-sleep rituals, such as setting intentions or journaling about specific ancestors. As they drift into sleep, they invite these ancestors to visit in dreams, bringing symbols, teachings, or insights that enrich their spiritual path. Upon waking, the seeker records these dreams, using their journal to capture patterns, symbols, and messages that can deepen their understanding of ancestral guidance. Over time, this practice sharpens the seeker's intuition and attunes them to the subtle language of dreams.

In "Ancestral Mantras and Chants," Metatron teaches the seeker how to use sound to connect with their lineage. Through specific chants or words passed down or created in reverence to ancestors, the seeker vibrates their intentions into the world, allowing sound to be the bridge between realms. The seeker may choose a simple phrase or create a melody, repeating it daily as a grounding ritual. These sounds, resonant with personal and ancestral frequencies, awaken the spirit of those who came before, calling forth strength, wisdom, and protection.

The seeker also engages in "Rituals of Ancestral Offering," where they set aside moments each week or month to give tangible offerings in honor of their lineage. Flowers, food, or incense are placed at the ancestral altar with words of gratitude and reverence. This act of giving serves to reinforce the spiritual connection and reminds the seeker of their responsibility to uphold and honor the legacy of those before them. Each offering is a pledge, a gesture that acknowledges the sacrifices and experiences of past generations, inviting harmony and blessing into the present.

In the practice of "Energetic Clearing of Ancestral Patterns," the seeker examines inherited patterns that may restrict growth or happiness. With Metatron's guidance, they identify these patterns, whether they manifest as limiting beliefs, recurring emotional cycles, or behavioral tendencies. Through visualization, they call upon Metatron's light to cleanse these energies, releasing ancestral burdens that no longer serve. This release is a transformative act, not only freeing the seeker but offering peace to ancestors whose own lives may have been marked by these same struggles. As old patterns dissolve, the seeker feels lighter, empowered to forge a path unburdened by the weight of inherited limitations.

Another ritual, "Communion through Sacred Texts and Symbols," allows the seeker to connect with their heritage through sacred objects, texts, or symbols relevant to their lineage. Metatron encourages the seeker to meditate upon these items, absorbing the energy and wisdom they contain. Whether they are family heirlooms, traditional texts, or cultural symbols, these objects carry vibrations of ancestral knowledge. In meditation, the seeker may hold or gaze upon these items, asking for guidance or simply inviting a deeper connection to the values and insights embedded within them.

In "Meditative Journey to Ancestral Lands," Metatron guides the seeker through a visualization that transports them to places of ancestral significance. Seated in quiet reflection, the seeker imagines themselves in landscapes or locations where their ancestors lived, worked, and thrived. As they walk these imagined paths, they sense the energy and presence of those who came before, absorbing the resilience, joy, and wisdom of their lives. This mental pilgrimage strengthens the seeker's bond to their heritage, instilling a sense of belonging and continuity that transcends time and space.

The "Cycle of Ancestral Forgiveness" is another profound exercise in this journey. The seeker is guided to forgive and release any ancestral actions or patterns that may carry emotional weight or unresolved energies. In a meditation, they visualize sending forgiveness and peace back through the lineage, healing unresolved conflicts, pain, or misunderstandings. This cycle of forgiveness becomes a blessing, allowing both the seeker and their ancestors to move forward with renewed peace and understanding, freeing future generations from carrying these energies.

Metatron introduces the "Invocation of Ancestral Strength," a practice that draws upon the resilience and virtues of those who came before. The seeker meditates, calling upon qualities they admire within their lineage—courage, compassion, wisdom, or creativity. With each invocation, they feel these qualities awakening within themselves, realizing that these virtues are part of their own spiritual inheritance. This practice empowers the seeker, allowing them to draw upon the strength of their ancestors to navigate challenges and manifest their highest potential.

Through these practices, the seeker's connection with ancestors transforms from abstract reverence into a living, interactive relationship. Metatron's guidance helps weave the past into the present, nurturing a lineage of wisdom, resilience, and love that empowers the seeker to walk their own path with purpose and pride. The journey through ancestral connection unfolds as a blessing, a sacred bond that continues to inspire and uplift, carrying the seeker forward with the strength of countless souls who walk beside them, unseen yet deeply felt.

Chapter 27
Overcoming Blockages

As the seeker progresses on their path of spiritual expansion, they inevitably encounter moments when energy feels stagnant or emotions seem heavy. These are the subtle signs of spiritual and emotional blockages—patterns or obstacles that lie hidden within, waiting to be unveiled and transformed. With Metatron's guidance, the seeker embarks on a journey inward, learning to identify these blockages, understand their origins, and find pathways to release them.

At the outset, Metatron teaches the seeker to become aware of the physical sensations that often signal a blockage: tension in certain areas of the body, feelings of heaviness, or even persistent discomforts that linger without physical cause. These sensations can reveal hidden emotional or energetic blockages. The seeker is encouraged to use mindful breathing as a way of focusing on these areas, paying attention to any emotions or memories that may arise as they explore these sensations.

In this journey of self-exploration, Metatron introduces "The Mirror of Self-Reflection." This practice involves a daily moment of introspection where the seeker looks within, examining their thoughts and emotions without judgment. By creating a ritual of self-reflection, the seeker becomes more aware of recurring feelings, unprocessed experiences, and patterns that may be quietly shaping their perceptions and decisions. This honest self-awareness is the first step toward transformation, allowing the seeker to observe and understand the root of their blockages.

To deepen this understanding, Metatron presents "The Path of Emotional Mapping." Here, the seeker draws upon memories and experiences from their past, identifying emotions tied to these events. With Metatron's energy as a guide, the seeker explores how past events might have left lingering impressions—perhaps a fear, an insecurity, or even self-doubt that limits growth. By gently exploring these connections, the seeker uncovers the origin of emotional patterns, recognizing them as energies that, though deeply ingrained, are not permanent.

Once the seeker identifies blockages, Metatron introduces "The Breath of Release." This practice involves a guided visualization where the seeker breathes deeply, imagining that each exhale carries out any stagnant or heavy energy they have uncovered. With each inhale, they invite Metatron's light into their being, envisioning it filling and healing the areas once occupied by the blockages. This visualization becomes a powerful ritual for releasing stored energy, creating a space within for peace and clarity to grow.

For blockages rooted in relationships or interactions with others, Metatron shares "The Ritual of Energetic Unbinding." Here, the seeker visualizes the ties that connect them to past experiences or people who may still hold an influence over their emotions. With compassion, they imagine gently severing these energetic ties, feeling a sense of freedom and lightness as they release them. This practice offers a sense of closure, allowing the seeker to move forward without carrying emotional residue from past relationships.

To maintain a balanced energy flow, Metatron introduces "The Flame of Transformation." In this meditative exercise, the seeker visualizes a flame—a pure, violet flame that symbolizes transformation and purification. They are encouraged to envision this flame absorbing any residual fears, anger, or sadness, transforming these energies into light and warmth. The Flame of Transformation purifies without judgment, reminding the seeker that all emotions, once released, become opportunities for healing and growth.

Recognizing that some blockages may come from subconscious fears or doubts, Metatron offers "The Journey of Self-Compassion." This practice invites the seeker to embrace their vulnerability, allowing any unresolved feelings to surface without fear or resistance. They are encouraged to speak words of kindness and acceptance to themselves, acknowledging that even their shadows are part of the journey. With each compassionate affirmation, the seeker's inner resilience strengthens, softening the resistance that blockages often build within.

For blockages that persist or feel deeply ingrained, Metatron introduces "The Light of Forgiveness." The seeker is guided to examine moments of pain, regret, or resentment and to gently offer forgiveness to themselves and others. This forgiveness is not a condoning of past actions but a release—a liberation of the energy that holds these experiences within. As forgiveness flows, the seeker feels a lightness returning to their being, as if burdens they once carried are now lifted and dissolved into Metatron's light.

Through "Chakra Alignment Meditation," the seeker finds a way to work directly with the body's energy centers. In this practice, they focus on each chakra, sensing any resistance, blockages, or disturbances that may linger there. With Metatron's presence, they visualize each chakra glowing with a radiant light, aligning and spinning in harmony, allowing blocked energy to flow freely once again. This meditation reconnects the seeker with their own source of vitality, grounding them in a state of balance and openness.

Lastly, Metatron shares "The Gift of Renewal Ritual," a final practice that invites the seeker to celebrate the release of blockages and the space now open for new energy. With gratitude, the seeker acknowledges their journey of healing and transformation, symbolizing it through an offering—perhaps a flower, a stone, or a written affirmation released into nature. This gesture becomes a closing ritual, a way of honoring the courage it took to confront and dissolve blockages that once seemed insurmountable.

As the seeker releases these inner constraints, they find themselves standing in a clearer light, feeling an expansion of their spirit and a deeper connection to their purpose. Metatron's guidance has shown them that every blockage, when met with understanding and patience, becomes an invitation for growth, a lesson in resilience, and a path toward true inner liberation.

In the journey of dissolving inner blockages, the seeker has already faced shadows within, illuminating hidden spaces with patience and understanding. Now, as Metatron's guidance deepens, the practices evolve, moving toward profound emotional release and lasting transformation. Here, the seeker is invited to work with specific rituals and techniques designed to confront remaining energetic constraints, freeing the spirit from any traces of doubt, fear, or past limitations.

Metatron begins by guiding the seeker to a practice known as "The Spiral of Release," a meditative journey where they visualize their life experiences spiraling before them. In this spiral, each event, feeling, or memory that holds weight or tension gently reveals itself. With Metatron's energy encircling them, the seeker visualizes each experience being absorbed into the spiral and transformed, dissolving into light. This process frees the soul from lingering burdens, allowing the seeker to move forward without the energetic remnants of past struggles.

As blockages are often reinforced by patterns of self-doubt, Metatron introduces "The Mirror of Affirmation." This exercise invites the seeker to stand before a mirror, connecting deeply with their own gaze. In this sacred space, they speak affirmations aloud—statements of self-acceptance, courage, and purpose that reverberate through their being. Each affirmation becomes a powerful tool to dismantle the voices of insecurity, empowering the seeker to see themselves as Metatron sees them: capable, worthy, and complete.

To aid in the release of emotional attachments, Metatron guides the seeker through "The Water Ceremony of Letting Go." In this ritual, the seeker prepares a bowl of pure water, symbolizing clarity and renewal. They are invited to hold this bowl while focusing on any lingering emotions—sadness, anger, regret—allowing these feelings to surface. As they release these emotions into the water, they sense the weight of each one dissolving. This ceremony becomes a living symbol of release, an outward act that reflects the cleansing within.

In situations where past wounds remain persistent, Metatron shares the practice of "Sacred Writing." Here, the seeker is encouraged to write a letter to themselves, detailing experiences or relationships that have left marks on their spirit. As they write, Metatron's energy surrounds them, infusing their words with healing and compassion. When the letter is complete, the seeker performs a ritual of release—either burning or burying the letter—symbolizing the completion of these experiences and the dissolution of their power over the present.

For deeper emotional liberation, Metatron introduces "The Heart Light Meditation." In this practice, the seeker closes their eyes, envisioning a warm, radiant light emanating from their heart chakra. This light flows through their entire being, gently reaching areas where past wounds might still linger. With each breath, the seeker visualizes this light healing and softening these places. They experience the gradual loosening of these blockages, feeling a new lightness within as their heart expands in acceptance and grace.

In addition, Metatron offers a tool for realigning the spirit through "The Sound of Release." Here, the seeker is invited to use their voice as an instrument of transformation, whether through chanting, humming, or simply vocalizing sounds that resonate with their current state. Each sound they create is infused with intention, carrying the energy of release and renewal. This vocal practice enables the seeker to shed old energies, leaving behind only the resonance of clarity and peace.

For blockages bound by fear, Metatron guides the seeker through "The Courage Stone Ritual." In this ritual, the seeker selects a stone, imbuing it with courage and intention. They are invited to hold the stone in moments of doubt, channeling any lingering fears into it. Over time, the stone becomes a vessel for these fears, absorbing and transforming them. When the seeker feels ready, they release the stone back to nature, symbolizing the surrender of these fears and the reclaiming of their inner strength.

For those who have difficulty letting go of old identities or past roles, Metatron presents "The Robe of Renewal." In a visualization, the seeker imagines themselves cloaked in a robe that represents all past versions of themselves—the roles they have played, the identities they once held. When they feel ready, they visualize gently removing this robe, leaving it behind as they step forward in their true essence. This act of letting go creates space for authenticity and self-discovery, allowing the seeker to honor the past while embracing their current self.

As the seeker progresses, Metatron introduces "The Dance of Liberation." Through music and movement, they release stored energy by allowing their body to move freely, guided by intuition. In this state, the seeker connects deeply with their physical form, letting emotions flow through movement. Each step, sway, or spin becomes an act of freedom, and each movement dismantles hidden blockages, allowing the energy within to flow unimpeded.

To close this journey of overcoming blockages, Metatron guides the seeker through "The Circle of Gratitude." In this final ritual, the seeker visualizes a circle of light around them, created by their own gratitude for each step, lesson, and challenge on their path. They take time to reflect on the growth achieved, thanking the parts of themselves they have released and the strength they have gained. This circle seals their experience, grounding them in a state of wholeness and balance.

In this space of gratitude, the seeker feels the gentle presence of Metatron, offering quiet affirmation of the transformations made. No longer bound by past limitations or fears, the seeker steps forward with clarity and courage, ready to explore new depths of spiritual awareness and personal freedom. The journey of release has opened within them a new landscape—one of harmony, potential, and true inner liberation.

Chapter 28
Spiritual Rebirth

In moments of profound introspection, when the past has been thoroughly examined and the spirit feels the pull toward something greater, the notion of spiritual rebirth emerges—a transformation as elusive as it is essential. Metatron gently introduces the reader to the possibility of rebirth, guiding the soul to shed outdated layers and rediscover its true essence. Rebirth, in the spiritual sense, is a journey that delves beyond mere change; it is a reawakening, a full-bodied return to the self's truest and most powerful form.

Metatron illuminates the ancient idea that spiritual rebirth is a path toward deeper consciousness, one where past experiences are integrated rather than erased, forming the foundation of wisdom and empathy. Just as the Phoenix rises renewed from ashes, so too can the soul, releasing the weight of its former patterns, identities, and limitations. This rebirth is an acknowledgment of the soul's resilience and adaptability, a process that allows for growth unrestrained by the confines of the past.

The journey of rebirth begins with an intimate practice called "Embracing the Void." Here, Metatron encourages the seeker to face an inner emptiness—a silence within—where all attachments and distractions are released, creating space for renewal. In meditation, the seeker descends into this quiet void, guided by Metatron's calming presence, until they reach a space of pure, unburdened stillness. It is here, in this sacred emptiness, that the first seeds of new growth take root.

One of the key aspects of spiritual rebirth is releasing attachment to old identities. To facilitate this, Metatron introduces "The Ceremony of Names," a practice wherein the seeker writes down names or labels they have identified with, be they roles, titles, or emotions—each one representing an aspect of a self that has now evolved. In a ritual of release, the seeker is invited to surrender each name, watching as it dissolves into light, signifying the release of attachments to outdated definitions of self. In the quiet aftermath, a new space is left open for the soul to redefine itself, without limitations.

In preparation for this transformation, Metatron introduces a profound visualization called "The Chrysalis." In this exercise, the seeker imagines themselves encased within a cocoon of light, safe and protected. Within this light, they undergo a transformative journey, shedding old patterns and limitations, just as a caterpillar metamorphoses into a butterfly. Within the chrysalis, they feel Metatron's guiding presence, allowing them to let go without fear and to trust the process of rebirth that is already unfolding within.

Spiritual rebirth also calls for a deep reconciliation with one's past, and Metatron encourages this through "The Garden of Memories" exercise. Here, the seeker envisions a garden filled with significant moments from their life—experiences, relationships, emotions, all arranged like flowers and stones in a landscape. As they walk through this garden, they revisit these moments, blessing each one with gratitude for the role it played. This compassionate acknowledgment transforms the memories, allowing them to be integrated as part of the seeker's journey rather than as weights pulling them backward.

Metatron also introduces "The Ritual of Reclaiming," a practice in which the seeker reflects upon aspects of themselves that may have been left behind or forgotten during life's challenges. Whether it's a sense of joy, a talent, or a dream, the seeker is guided to reclaim these parts, welcoming them back as vital elements of their reborn self. With each aspect reclaimed, they feel a renewed sense of wholeness, as if each piece of their soul has been lovingly restored.

Metatron guides the seeker through "The Breath of Renewal," a breathing exercise that purifies and revitalizes the soul. Through deep, intentional breaths, the seeker envisions breathing in the energy of new beginnings, and with each exhale, they release energies and beliefs that no longer serve them. This rhythm of breathing becomes a source of strength and clarity, grounding them in the present moment as they prepare to step into a new phase of spiritual existence.

The seeker is introduced to "The Symbol of Rebirth." In this practice, Metatron invites them to discover or create a personal symbol that represents their rebirth journey. This symbol becomes a reminder of the new path they are embarking upon, a powerful anchor that holds the energy of transformation. Whether it's a simple shape, an animal, or a personal drawing, the symbol serves as a touchstone of renewal that the seeker can return to whenever they need to realign with their reborn self.

As the seeker stands poised at the threshold of rebirth, guided by Metatron's unwavering presence, they feel a surge of vitality, a quiet but profound conviction that the journey of transformation is theirs to embrace fully. The past has become part of their strength, and the future glimmers with possibility, unshackled and expansive. This moment of rebirth is an invitation to embody all they have learned, to live with clarity, and to embrace the world with open arms, as a soul renewed and reborn.

One of the core practices for integrating rebirth is "The Mirror of the True Self." Here, the seeker is guided to sit before a mirror, meeting their own gaze with openness and compassion. Metatron encourages them to look past the surface, beyond external appearances, to connect with the essence within—the self unburdened by past expectations and free from future projections. In this reflective practice, the seeker recognizes their spiritual nature, beholding the timeless soul that has emerged from transformation. With Metatron's presence, they are invited to accept and honor this self, making a silent commitment to live in alignment with their renewed purpose.

Moving deeper, Metatron introduces the "Prayer of New Beginnings," a ritual that calls upon the energies of the universe to bless and support the journey ahead. This prayer is not merely words, but an invocation of the seeker's intentions and a call for divine alignment. In this prayer, they release any lingering doubts or attachments, allowing the energy of pure potential to flow through them. The words resonate as a vibration, creating a sense of connection with the universe, affirming that their rebirth is not only personal but an alignment with the larger forces at play.

To ground their reborn self in the physical world, the seeker is led through "The Ritual of Sacred Earth." In this ritual, Metatron guides them to plant a seed or nurture a young plant, representing the new life taking root within. This act of care becomes a symbol of the seeker's journey, as they tend to this growing life with the same dedication they give to their spiritual growth. Each time they water the plant or feel its leaves under their fingers, they are reminded of their own rebirth and the care required to sustain it. The physical act becomes a grounding force, anchoring their transformation in the physical realm.

Metatron then reveals "The Circle of Light," a visualization where the seeker envisions themselves encircled by a ring of light—pure, radiant, and endless. Within this circle, they are held in safety, protected from the energetic patterns of the past. Here, the seeker releases any residual energies or patterns that no longer align with their reborn self, letting them dissolve into the light. This practice creates a sacred boundary, a space where only what aligns with their new state of being can enter. Each time they return to this visualization, they feel a renewed sense of clarity, a reminder that they are held by the universe, secure and grounded in their rebirth.

As the seeker moves through these rituals, Metatron introduces "The Path of the Heart," an exercise in which the seeker is encouraged to make choices based on the pure guidance of the heart. In daily decisions, they are asked to pause, place a hand on their heart, and feel into the wisdom that resides there. In this quiet moment, they ask themselves whether their choice aligns with their reborn spirit. This practice transforms even small, everyday decisions into acts of alignment, making the process of rebirth an ongoing reality rather than a single event.

"The Phoenix Breath" is another practice introduced by Metatron, which involves intentional breathwork to foster resilience and openness. In this practice, the seeker breathes deeply, visualizing themselves as a Phoenix, inhaling the energy of transformation and exhaling any remaining shadows or resistance. This breath becomes a reminder of their resilience, a testament to the cycles of release and renewal that their spirit has embraced. Each breath draws them closer to embodying the vitality and power of their reborn self, reinforcing the journey as one of continuous growth.

Metatron guides the seeker through "The Journal of Emergence," a reflective practice of writing down insights, moments of clarity, and signs of growth. This journal becomes a sacred space where the seeker can explore their thoughts, noting how their perception of life has evolved. It is in these pages that they capture the essence of their transformation, recording both the subtle shifts and the profound changes. With each entry, they observe the unfolding of their rebirth, finding strength in their own words and charting their progress toward a life lived in true alignment.

As the seeker stands within a new reality—one where they have fully integrated the experiences of transformation—they are no longer bound by the shadows of the past, now carrying forward the light of their rebirth. With Metatron's guidance, they step into this new life with grace, grounded in self-knowledge and embraced by the limitless possibilities that lie ahead. They are a being reborn, poised to navigate the world with clarity, compassion, and unwavering inner strength.

Chapter 29
Wisdom Integration

At the heart of spiritual transformation lies a subtle, yet profound, task: integrating the wisdom gathered along the journey. Under the guidance of Metatron, the seeker begins to weave the insights, practices, and revelations into the fabric of everyday life, deepening their understanding of integration—not as a separate act, but as a way of living where each choice, interaction, and intention becomes an expression of their spiritual truth.

Metatron introduces "The Daily Alignment Ritual," a simple yet powerful practice designed to ground the seeker's energy each morning. Upon waking, the seeker places a hand over the heart, breathing deeply and attuning to the core intentions of peace, clarity, and presence. Through this ritual, the connection with Metatron's energy is re-established each day, creating a steady foundation from which all other experiences flow. This practice serves as a gentle reminder that spiritual wisdom is not meant to be reserved for sacred spaces alone but to be carried into every moment.

Following this, Metatron guides the seeker through "The Spiral of Reflection." This meditative practice invites the reader to revisit significant moments from their journey, exploring how challenges, insights, and spiritual awakenings have shaped them. By tracing these moments, the seeker begins to see patterns in their growth, recognizing the wisdom gained from experiences that once seemed disparate. In reflecting on these patterns, they find renewed gratitude and clarity, noticing how each stage of their journey has led seamlessly to the next, like a spiral ascending toward a higher understanding.

To deepen the wisdom integration further, Metatron introduces "The Path of Kindness," which emphasizes applying spiritual insights in practical, compassionate ways. The seeker is encouraged to engage in acts of kindness—whether through words, gestures, or simple attentiveness to others. This practice transforms spiritual wisdom from abstract knowledge into a living expression, allowing the seeker to act as a vessel for positive energy in the world. Each act of kindness reinforces their connection to the divine, embedding their spiritual journey within the context of human connection and empathy.

In "The Balance of Receiving and Giving," Metatron emphasizes the importance of harmony in energy flow. The seeker is guided to reflect on where their energy is directed, observing whether they are overextending in service or holding back out of self-preservation. This practice encourages an openness to both giving and receiving, acknowledging that the wisdom of the journey is sustained through balance. Metatron reminds the seeker that the natural flow of energy—like the ocean's tides—is cyclical, nurturing both the self and the collective. By honoring this rhythm, the seeker embraces wisdom as a state of balance, where the divine and earthly realms intertwine.

Another central practice is "The Candle of Intention." Each evening, the seeker lights a small candle, focusing on a specific intention, whether it is gratitude, peace, or clarity. This flame serves as a tangible representation of their inner light, burning steadily through life's uncertainties. Metatron guides them to sit quietly with the candle's glow, reflecting on the day and how their actions aligned with their spiritual path. This simple ritual invites moments of self-awareness and nurtures a habit of contemplation, allowing the wisdom of their journey to settle and expand within.

"The Practice of Inner Dialogue" is introduced as a way for the seeker to maintain an open conversation with their inner self. Here, they are encouraged to ask themselves questions about their desires, choices, and responses, allowing the wisdom gained from the journey to inform their answers. Through this dialogue, they develop a compassionate self-awareness, understanding how their actions align or misalign with their spiritual values. This practice cultivates a deeper understanding of themselves as dynamic beings, able to adapt, grow, and refine their actions to stay aligned with their truth.

To complete this journey, Metatron shares "The Vision of Life as a Whole," a visualization practice in which the seeker envisions their life as a complete, interconnected landscape. They are guided to see every experience, relationship, and aspiration as a piece of a larger mosaic, each one essential to the beauty of the whole. In this vision, they sense the interconnectedness of every lesson, the wisdom woven into their life, and how every moment is a step in their spiritual evolution. With Metatron's guidance, they perceive that each day is an opportunity to embody the fullness of their journey, merging past wisdom with present purpose.

As they arrive at this new state of awareness, the journey transforms from a sequence of practices into a way of being. With every breath, choice, and intention, they embody the wisdom that Metatron has helped cultivate, moving forward with clarity and peace, integrated into the wholeness of their spirit.

The unfolding of wisdom brings the seeker to a heightened awareness of life's subtle teachings, illuminating how to weave spiritual insights into a seamless practice. Metatron's guidance deepens this integration, helping the seeker create a sacred foundation that extends beyond rituals and resides within their every interaction. Through practices that honor their path and build resilience, the seeker enters this final phase of wisdom integration, forging a bridge between the profound and the practical.

Metatron introduces "The Sacred Thread of Presence," a meditation that roots the seeker in the present moment. In this exercise, they learn to bring their awareness into the here and now, embracing each experience with openheartedness. The Sacred Thread represents an inner commitment to live with attention, cultivating a grounded state that remains unaffected by external turbulence. This practice is not an escape from life's challenges but a way to see them with clarity, grounded in a wisdom that perceives beyond appearances. Through daily practice, presence becomes the guiding thread that weaves spiritual understanding into the fabric of life.

To support this sense of groundedness, Metatron introduces "The Circle of Resilience." This ritual empowers the seeker to draw upon their inner strength, even when faced with moments of doubt or hardship. They are guided to envision a circle of light surrounding them, representing their strength and the accumulation of wisdom they've gathered on their journey. The Circle of Resilience is a reminder of their intrinsic power, fortified by each step of the path they have walked. By activating this circle, they can stand firm and centered, protected by the unwavering presence of their own spiritual essence.

An essential part of this journey is "The Ritual of Release." Here, Metatron invites the seeker to examine attachments that may hinder their journey forward. Through an introspective exercise, they reflect on past experiences, relationships, or fears that no longer serve their spiritual growth. This ritual allows them to let go, honoring what has passed and embracing the freedom of release. Metatron's light supports this transition, dissolving lingering energies and creating space for new growth. The Ritual of Release becomes a powerful tool in maintaining clarity and openness, allowing wisdom to continuously evolve without the constraints of past burdens.

Another practice, "The Heart of Compassion," emphasizes the role of empathy and understanding in spiritual wisdom. In this exercise, the seeker is guided to view others through a lens of compassion, seeing beyond behaviors to the inherent divinity within each individual. Metatron teaches that wisdom is magnified through acts of compassion, bridging the distance between individuals and creating a flow of shared understanding.

By embracing compassion as a natural extension of their wisdom, the seeker radiates a gentle, transformative energy that affects all they encounter, fostering harmony and deep connection.

To further embed wisdom in daily life, Metatron introduces "The Reflection of Gratitude," a journaling practice that focuses on cultivating a mindset of thankfulness. Each evening, the seeker reflects on the day's experiences, recognizing moments where wisdom revealed itself, whether through challenges overcome, lessons learned, or simple acts of kindness. This practice of gratitude strengthens their connection to the divine by acknowledging the continuous flow of blessings. Gratitude becomes a lens through which they view life, reinforcing a state of fulfillment and contentment rooted in the journey's many gifts.

In "The Echo of Intuition," Metatron encourages the seeker to trust and develop their inner voice, a source of wisdom that resonates from within. This practice involves moments of quiet reflection, where they tune into their intuition, listening to its subtle guidance. By honoring this inner wisdom, the seeker learns to navigate life with a sense of trust and confidence, guided not only by what they've learned but by an inner knowing that transcends reason. Metatron's presence strengthens their connection to intuition, helping them recognize and heed the gentle nudges that lead them closer to their true path.

This journey culminates in "The Practice of Continuous Alignment," a ritual that embodies the cumulative teachings shared along the way. In this exercise, the seeker envisions their chakras aligned and flowing with energy, each center radiating the lessons and energies cultivated through their journey with Metatron. By visualizing this alignment, they create a state of unity within themselves, where mind, body, and spirit harmonize effortlessly. This continuous alignment practice becomes a touchstone—a way to recalibrate, reconnect, and reaffirm their commitment to a life lived in wisdom.

As the seeker steps into this space of wholeness, they embody the wisdom of each moment of insight. The journey has transformed them, weaving spiritual knowledge into an enduring, harmonious way of life. With Metatron as an eternal guide, they walk forward with courage, compassion, and unwavering clarity, prepared to embrace whatever lies ahead with the wisdom of their soul's deepest truths.

Chapter 30
Peace and Contentment

The journey toward inner peace leads the seeker into a state of gentle, profound contentment—a space within the soul that hums with harmony, no matter what the outer world may bring. Archangel Metatron introduces pathways to cultivate inner peace, guiding the seeker to explore the subtle art of accepting and embracing each moment. This practice is not about escaping reality but discovering a wellspring of tranquility within, a peace that emerges as the seeker aligns with their true self and the flow of the universe.

Metatron begins with "The Breath of Stillness," a meditation that draws the seeker's awareness to the simplicity and grounding power of their own breath. In this practice, the seeker learns to tune into the rhythm of breathing, finding that each inhale and exhale serves as a reminder of life's natural flow. By focusing on the breath, they center themselves, drawing away from distractions and anxieties. The Breath of Stillness brings them back to their essence, creating a sacred space within where peace exists unconditionally, untouched by the noise of the external world.

Following this, Metatron introduces "The Embrace of Acceptance." In this practice, the seeker is guided to let go of the resistance to life's unfolding events and to welcome all experiences, even the uncomfortable ones, as part of the divine journey. Acceptance is not passive but an active embrace, a way of meeting life with openness and trust in the underlying wisdom of every situation. Metatron encourages the seeker to view each moment as a teacher, offering insight and growth. Through acceptance, they release the grip of expectations, fears, and attachments, creating room for a peaceful heart that flows with life's natural rhythm.

Another integral practice is "The Path of Gratitude for the Present." In this exercise, the seeker learns to focus on what is present and true in the current moment. Through a daily ritual of gratitude, they honor even the simplest joys—a morning sunrise, a shared smile, or a moment of quiet reflection. Metatron teaches that gratitude amplifies contentment, showing the seeker that fulfillment does not depend on future achievements or possessions but is found in embracing the abundance of the here and now. This gratitude practice builds a strong foundation of inner peace, guiding the seeker to see the richness of life just as it is.

In "The Mirror of Self-Compassion," Metatron leads the seeker to turn a gentle gaze inward, cultivating compassion for themselves. Through a meditative visualization, they are encouraged to release self-criticism and embrace the beauty of their own journey, honoring both strengths and vulnerabilities. Metatron shows them that peace blossoms when they treat themselves with the same compassion and understanding they offer others. In this self-compassion, they find a refuge, a place where they can rest and rejuvenate, free from judgment or expectations, held in the warmth of their own acceptance.

Another essential part of this journey is "The Sanctuary of Silence," a practice that encourages the seeker to set aside moments for stillness and quietude. In these times of silence, they connect with the deep well of peace that lies within. Metatron explains that silence is a doorway to the sacred, a way to listen to the whispers of the soul and the gentle guidance of the divine. The Sanctuary of Silence teaches the seeker to find peace not only in meditation but also in the pauses of daily life, transforming even small moments of quiet into profound opportunities for spiritual alignment.

Another essential practice, "The Flow of Forgiveness," guides the seeker to release resentment and past wounds that may disrupt their peace. With Metatron's support, they are encouraged to approach forgiveness as a path to freedom, understanding that releasing the weight of grievances opens space for tranquility to fill the heart. This exercise does not rush forgiveness but invites a gentle letting go, honoring the pain while choosing to rise above it. As they forgive, the seeker liberates themselves, finding that true peace is rooted not only in accepting life but also in releasing what no longer serves the soul's growth.

In "The Illumination of Joy," Metatron leads the seeker to recognize moments of simple happiness, encouraging them to see joy as a state of being rather than a fleeting feeling. Through a guided visualization, the seeker connects with a source of inner light—a spark of joy that is ever-present, regardless of circumstances. This joy is a reminder of their divine essence, an inner glow that sustains them. The Illumination of Joy encourages them to celebrate life, to see the beauty in small moments, and to recognize that peace and contentment are deeply intertwined with the capacity to experience and cherish joy.

Metatron completes this journey with "The Practice of Surrender." Here, the seeker learns the art of surrendering to the divine flow, relinquishing the need for control and allowing life to unfold naturally. Surrender is not about giving up; it is a profound trust in the wisdom of the universe. Metatron guides the seeker to see surrender as a sacred act, a way of aligning with a higher purpose. In this state, peace flows effortlessly, as they release the weight of worries and rest in the assurance that all is held within the divine order.

As the seeker integrates these practices, they come to understand that peace and contentment are not distant goals but qualities that reside within, waiting to be nurtured and expressed. Metatron's guidance leads them to a profound realization: that peace is an ever-present state, accessible at any moment when one chooses to step into alignment with their true self and the divine. In this space, they discover that contentment arises from within, a quiet joy that accompanies them through all seasons of life, illuminating the path with gentle grace.

With each passing lesson, the seeker grows more attuned to the stillness within, cultivating a sanctuary of peace and an enduring sense of contentment. This journey builds upon the practices already established, leading the seeker further into techniques for sustaining this inner state as a core part of daily life. Here, Archangel Metatron introduces additional, subtle layers of practice to deepen the peace and contentment that flow from spiritual alignment, anchoring the soul in a state of serene, unshakable balance.

Metatron begins with "Grounding in Divine Presence," a practice that centers the seeker within the vastness of divine energy. Through this grounding exercise, the seeker learns to embody the energy of peace as a foundation, allowing it to flow from their roots, extending through the earth and sky alike. This connection to divine presence becomes an anchor in times of inner or outer turbulence. As they focus on their breath and visualize themselves as deeply rooted, they become more stable, drawing on the energy of the Earth and cosmos to remain steady. Metatron guides them to feel that they are part of a vast, interconnected whole, and in this union with the divine, they find peace as a living, breathing force.

Another practice, "Heart-Centered Awareness," draws the seeker into a deeper awareness of the heart chakra, a center of love and compassion. Metatron leads them to feel each heartbeat as a pulse of peace, encouraging them to carry this awareness into their interactions with others. This practice shows that peace is not only an internal state but can be expressed outwardly through kindness and mindful communication. By embracing heart-centered awareness, they learn to respond to the world with gentle strength, creating harmony in their relationships and environment. In this way, the heart becomes both a sanctuary and a source, radiating peace that reaches all who come into contact with it.

In "Vision of Inner Sanctuary," Metatron introduces a visualization of a sacred inner place, a space where the seeker can retreat at any time for renewal and solitude. This sanctuary is envisioned as a peaceful landscape, perhaps a quiet forest or a calm beach, filled with symbols of the seeker's personal path. The Vision of Inner Sanctuary becomes a refuge, a place they can return to in meditation, where peace is always accessible and abundant. In moments of tension, the seeker is encouraged to close their eyes, breathe deeply, and reconnect with this sanctuary, allowing it to replenish and ground them. Through repeated visits to this inner place, they reinforce the habit of finding peace within, regardless of life's outer circumstances.

Metatron then shares "The Ritual of Presence," a mindful approach to daily actions. In this ritual, the seeker learns to infuse simple tasks—whether eating, walking, or working—with focused, peaceful awareness. This practice teaches that peace and contentment are not limited to meditation or solitude but can be woven into every part of life. By performing daily actions with full presence, the seeker awakens to the beauty and meaning within the ordinary, discovering contentment in the smallest details. The Ritual of Presence deepens their connection to the world, creating a rhythm of peace that flows seamlessly between inner stillness and outward action.

Next, Metatron introduces "Transcending Duality," an advanced practice that encourages the seeker to embrace life's contrasts without being swayed by them. This exercise teaches that peace arises not from denying life's dualities—joy and sorrow, gain and loss—but from accepting them as essential elements of the human journey. Metatron guides the seeker to observe these opposites without attachment, cultivating a witness consciousness that remains steady regardless of the external situation. Through transcending duality, they find a peace that is beyond circumstance, a contentment that flows from embracing the fullness of existence. This practice strengthens resilience, allowing the seeker to navigate life with grace, understanding that every experience, whether light or shadow, serves their growth.

In "Daily Harmonization with Divine Light," the seeker learns a practice of morning and evening alignment with

Metatron's energy. By starting the day with a brief visualization of light flowing through each chakra, they set an intention for peace and protection that carries them through daily challenges. At night, they close with gratitude, visualizing light that surrounds and restores their energy as they rest. This harmonization becomes a gentle but powerful routine, helping them maintain spiritual alignment and peace throughout the day. With each sunrise and sunset, they renew their connection to divine light, reinforcing their commitment to live from a place of balance and serenity.

The journey continues with "Forging Peace through Surrender." In this profound practice, Metatron guides the seeker to release the need to control life's unfolding, allowing divine wisdom to lead the way. Through an act of surrender, they learn to trust the unseen patterns of existence, letting go of resistance. Forging Peace through Surrender does not mean passive acceptance but an empowered choice to flow with life. As they practice this surrender, they find that the burdens of worry and fear dissolve, replaced by an expansive feeling of freedom. This act of release transforms peace into a living presence within, one that adapts to all situations with quiet strength and trust.

Metatron introduces "Embracing Sacred Stillness," a practice that calls for deeper periods of silence and contemplation, inviting the seeker to listen to the subtle voice of the soul. Sacred stillness goes beyond moments of quiet; it is a space where the soul connects directly with divine wisdom, finding answers and peace that are beyond words. In this stillness, the seeker feels the pulse of creation itself, an underlying rhythm that guides all beings. Through moments of silent communion, they come to know peace not as an idea but as an experience, a tangible connection to the vast intelligence of the universe. Sacred stillness becomes a sanctuary where the seeker renews their sense of purpose, emerging with clarity and contentment that remains with them long after.

As these practices take root, the seeker begins to live from a place of profound, embodied peace, radiating contentment to all around them. Metatron's guidance here creates a foundation that anchors them, nurturing a soul that is balanced, compassionate, and deeply aligned. The seeker's heart becomes a vessel of peace, and their life a testament to the quiet strength that arises when one is truly at peace with the self and the universe.

Chapter 31
Final Connection

A path walked with intention often leads to transformation that is profound and lasting. As the reader approaches the end of this spiritual journey with Archangel Metatron, there is a pause—a moment to recognize and reflect on all the shifts, revelations, and awakenings experienced along the way. Here, a contemplative return to the heart of the journey invites revisiting the wisdom that has guided each step. Under Metatron's attentive presence, the seeker now stands at a precipice where past insights and new beginnings intertwine, ready to deepen their commitment to their spiritual path.

Metatron invites the reader to recall the initial connection with divine energy established in the book's early sections. Through guided introspection, the seeker traces the journey back to that foundational alignment, observing how this connection has grown and strengthened. Here, they are encouraged to see their progress not only in the external shifts but in the subtleties of their inner world. This phase of self-reflection reveals how past doubts have softened, how once-dormant potentials have flourished, and how resilience has taken root.

In "Mirror of the Soul," Metatron guides the reader to gaze into their spiritual essence, as though looking into a clear, quiet lake reflecting their true self. Through this exercise, they see the layers of identity—the roles, experiences, and beliefs—dissolve into a deeper sense of pure awareness. The Mirror of the Soul practice is an invitation to embrace all parts of the journey without judgment. Here, the seeker finds peace with both their shadows and their light, understanding that every aspect has played a role in their spiritual unfolding. In this space, self-acceptance becomes the doorway to a fuller, more expansive vision of self.

A practice called "Gratitude Revisited" leads the seeker through a sequence of meditative reflections, revisiting the moments that have brought learning, healing, or grace. Metatron guides them to express gratitude for each phase of their spiritual growth, acknowledging even the struggles and challenges as vital parts of the whole. Through gratitude, they witness the interconnectedness of each step, realizing that each experience has woven a tapestry of spiritual resilience. Gratitude Revisited fosters a heartfelt recognition of the ways in which the soul has been shaped, encouraging the reader to look upon their journey as a sacred gift, full of both mystery and purpose.

As the reader stands poised to continue their journey beyond this book, Metatron introduces "Sealing the Connection." In this ritual, the seeker visualizes a golden light emanating from their heart, a light that encompasses every lesson, every insight, and every transformation experienced. This golden light forms an energetic seal, creating an unbreakable connection to the divine wisdom within. Sealing the Connection is more than a ritual; it is a conscious choice to carry forward the sacred insights gained, to keep the doors of spiritual growth open, and to honor the bond with Metatron as a lifelong guide. The seeker is reminded that this connection, once formed, will endure, providing a constant source of inner strength and guidance.

In "Vision of the Path Ahead," Metatron invites the reader to visualize their spiritual path unfolding before them, a path illuminated with purpose and possibility. This is not a path bound by rigid goals or expectations; rather, it is one of openness, where each step is an opportunity to grow and align with divine truth. Metatron guides them to release any need for certainty about the future, allowing trust to lead the way. Through this visualization, they feel the energy of their spiritual mission—an energy that will continue to evolve as they evolve, bringing new insights, teachers, and companions along the way.

In "Return to the Heart," the reader is encouraged to reconnect with the essence of who they are, the spark of divinity within that has been there since the beginning. In this practice, Metatron leads them to envision their heart as a sacred vessel, one that holds all they have encountered and embraced on this journey. The Return to the Heart practice is a reminder that, at its core, spirituality is about love—love for self, others, and the divine essence that unites all. Here, they find peace, contentment, and a profound sense of wholeness, knowing that they have everything they need within.

As Metatron's guidance comes to a close, the seeker is left with an invitation to continue, to explore further, and to live from this newfound alignment. With each breath, they carry forward the sacred teachings, not as distant memories but as vibrant truths within their very being. The journey, though filled with moments of learning, challenge, and enlightenment, is not over. It continues with every step, shaped by the wisdom cultivated and the commitment made. In this quiet moment of reflection, they stand connected—both to themselves and to the divine—ready to embrace the path ahead with a spirit full of light and an open, grateful heart.

In the quiet space where the journey concludes, there emerges a profound awareness that this ending is but a beginning. Metatron's presence, a radiant and compassionate guide, lingers with warmth, offering the reader a final blessing—a gesture of eternal support and encouragement for the path that continues beyond these pages. Here, the seeker stands, enveloped in the light of wisdom gathered through each part of their journey, ready to embrace the life that awaits with an open heart and spirit.

A final ritual, "The Covenant of Light," marks this moment. Metatron leads the reader through a meditation in which they envision a golden circle surrounding them, connecting earth and sky, body and spirit, in a unified field of energy. Within this sacred space, they feel the essence of their spiritual journey: the trials overcome, the revelations discovered, and the transformation achieved. The Covenant of Light is an invitation to make a commitment—a pledge to nurture the wisdom that has blossomed within, to honor the truths learned, and to walk forward with a heart aligned to purpose. It is a vow to stay true to one's spiritual path, with Metatron's presence as a beacon of guidance.

In a practice called "Embracing the Divine Path," the seeker reflects on the themes that have woven through their spiritual journey: balance, compassion, clarity, resilience, and love. Metatron encourages them to see how these qualities are now part of their very being, natural guides that will support them in navigating life's ongoing mysteries. Each theme is like a radiant gemstone embedded in the fabric of the reader's soul, a reminder of their growth and the wisdom gained. They are reminded that each step forward is an opportunity to deepen these qualities, to grow ever more attuned to their inner self and the divine energy that flows through all things.

In "Unity with All," the reader is invited to expand their awareness beyond the personal journey and feel their place within the vast web of existence. Metatron leads them to see their connection not only to the divine but to the collective spirit that unites all beings. Through this meditation, they sense a profound bond with others who walk spiritual paths, as well as with the Earth, the stars, and the cosmos. Unity with All instills a sense of purpose that extends beyond the self, a calling to live in harmony and contribute to the collective evolution of consciousness.

Metatron imparts a blessing in "The Eternal Flame," a practice in which the reader visualizes a flame ignited in their heart, a flame that burns brightly and cannot be extinguished. This flame represents the divine spark within, an eternal light of truth, compassion, and resilience. The Eternal Flame is a reminder that no matter where life leads, this light will be with them, a constant source of strength and guidance. Through this flame, they are forever connected to the divine, and in moments of doubt, they need only look within to find clarity and courage.

With this final connection, Metatron steps back, not as an absence but as a gentle shift, allowing the seeker to stand independently on their spiritual path, strengthened and illuminated by the journey they have undertaken. The reader is left with a deep sense of peace, an inner knowing that they carry everything they need within. They have learned to trust their inner wisdom, to find joy in spiritual practice, and to view life as an ever-unfolding journey of growth and revelation.

In this quiet conclusion, the seeker feels whole, aligned, and ready for what lies beyond, armed with the tools, practices, and understanding to continue walking a path of light. The journey has come full circle, each lesson and practice seamlessly integrated into the spirit, ready to be lived and embodied. As they turn the final page, they step forward, empowered and blessed, forever connected to Metatron, to the divine, and to the boundless wisdom that resides within.

Epilogue

Upon reaching the end of this journey, you are no longer the same as when you began. Each teaching, each practice, and each meditation offered by Metatron has shaped your consciousness in a way that ordinary words could hardly convey. You have learned to walk the path between the realms of the tangible and the spiritual, and, more than that, you have discovered that this journey continues in every act, thought, and sensation.

With every page, it was as if layers of reality and of yourself were revealed, dissolving old limiting beliefs, clarifying your intentions, and strengthening your purpose. Metatron has guided you along a path of alignment, helping to restore balance between mind, body, and spirit so that now you possess a deeper understanding of your own energy centers. From this point on, your journey advances towards what Metatron has shown as one of life's greatest secrets: the power of presence.

The spiritual practice inspired by Metatron does not end here; it blossoms, leading you to integrate these teachings into everyday life. This learning is a reminder that true protection, healing, and growth come from a genuine connection with the essence of all that is. In each moment of introspection, each small pause, you relive this state of harmony, of realignment with universal energy.

You have been invited to explore your energy centers as never before, transforming them into gateways that expand your perception and strengthen your connection with the divine. This inner journey reiterates that spirituality is not an escape from life's challenges but a path to face them with serenity, self-compassion, and wisdom. The energy now circulating freely within you carries the potential to impact the world around you, creating a wave of transformation that begins within and extends to everyone you encounter.

Metatron has gifted you with a holistic vision of existence, revealing that each being is a unique spark of a greater force and that, when aligned, this spark radiates light and love in all it touches. This vision awakens both the responsibility and the honor of living with authenticity and openness. You now understand that your spiritual path is an act of service, a sharing of the peace and harmony you have achieved with all those around you.

As you close this book, carry with you the wisdom that spirituality is a continuous journey. Each conscious breath is an opportunity to reconnect with the divine essence, to remember that you are, simultaneously, part of something immeasurable and essential in your singularity. Metatron will be with you every step forward, your guardian and guide, inspiring the expansion of this consciousness as you choose each day to align with your inner truth.

This epilogue is not a farewell but an opening for new experiences, an invitation to continue expanding your spiritual journey. Take the knowledge you've gained and let it flourish in your actions so that your strengthened light may not only illuminate your own path but also the lives of those you encounter. With each breath, in every thought, may the hidden power of your essence continue to unfold.

www.ingramcontent.com/pod-product-compliance
Lightning Source LLC
LaVergne TN
LVHW040051080526
838202LV00045B/3583